Company Barbour Brothers, Mary E Bradford

A Treatise on Lace-Making

embroidery and needle-work with Irish flax threads - Vol. 2

Company Barbour Brothers, Mary E Bradford

A Treatise on Lace-Making
embroidery and needle-work with Irish flax threads - Vol. 2

ISBN/EAN: 9783337126209

Printed in Europe, USA, Canada, Australia, Japan

Cover: Foto ©Andreas Hilbeck / pixelio.de

More available books at **www.hansebooks.com**

BOOK NO. 2.

BARBOUR'S

PRIZE NEEDLE-WORK SERIES.

A TREATISE

ON

LACE-MAKING, EMBROIDERY, AND NEEDLE-WORK

WITH

IRISH FLAX THREAD.

THIRD EDITION.

PUBLISHED BY

THE BARBOUR BROTHERS COMPANY.

1895.

PRESS OF
Rockwell and Churchill,
BOSTON.

Explanation of terms used in knitting and crocheting will be found on page 130.

Directions for washing Embroidery, on page 131.

This book is 3d edition of No. 2, issued October, 1895.

BOOKS No. 1, No. 3, AND No. 4,

AND

BOOK OF INSTRUCTION FOR MACRAMÉ LACE MAKING

are still in print, and will be sent to any address upon receipt of ten
cents each.   In addition to Patterns for work, they contain general
directions for Crocheting, Knitting, Antique or Guipure Lace, Darned
or Embroidered Net, Tatting, Embroidery, and instructions how to
properly wash Embroidery and Tatting.

If consumers find difficulty in procuring Barbour's Linen Thread
from their local stores, it will be sent from The Barbour Brothers
Company, New York, to any address, postage paid, upon receipt of
stamps or silver, as follows :

3-cord, 200-yards spools, dark blue, white, whited
    brown (or ecru), and drabs . . . . . . 10 cents ea. spool.
3-cord, carpet thread, any color 5   "   " skein.
00 Ulster rope linen floss, any color, 80 shades . 5   "   "   "
No. 4. etching flax, any color, 80 shades . . . 5   "   2 skeins.
Crochet thread, balls, gray, cream, and white.
    Nos. 16, 18, 20, and 25 . . . . 15 cents per ball.
    Nos. 30, 35, 40, and 50   . . . 20   "   "   "
    Nos. 60 and 70 25   "   "   "

PUBLISHERS' NOTICE.

In placing before the public our Book " No. 2," we ask for it the same kind and cordial interest that was so generally extended to our " No. 1," and which made its sale large, and the competition for prizes so successful — as is shown by the following circular announcing the award of prizes :

Nov. 21, 1891.

In issuing the report of the Committee of Ladies who have made the Award of Prizes for Needle-work, as offered in " BARBOUR'S PRIZE NEEDLE-WORK SERIES, No. 1," it may be interesting to know that Linen Thread Needle-work, of beautiful design and pattern, was received from ladies residing in the following States :

ALABAMA.	KENTUCKY.	NEW HAMPSHIRE.
CONNECTICUT.	MISSOURI.	OREGON.
CALIFORNIA.	MASSACHUSETTS.	OHIO.
COLORADO.	MARYLAND.	PENNSYLVANIA.
FLORIDA.	MINNESOTA.	SOUTH DAKOTA.
GEORGIA.	MICHIGAN.	TENNESSEE.
IDAHO.	MAINE.	TEXAS.
ILLINOIS.	NORTH CAROLINA.	VIRGINIA.
IOWA.	NEW JERSEY.	VERMONT.
INDIANA.	NEW YORK.	WISCONSIN.
KANSAS.	NEBRASKA.	WASHINGTON.

AWARD OF PRIZES.

1. — 1st Prize, Miss Carrie V. Wildey, 152 Keap Street, Brooklyn, E. D., N. Y.

   2d Prize, Mrs. Charles Goff, Middlebury, Addison Co., Vt.

2. — 1st Prize, Mrs. H. W. Howland, Xenia, Clay Co., Ill.

   2d Prize, Mrs. Melissa Mitchell, Russellville, E. Tenn.

3. — 1st Prize, Miss Alice Hinckley, Box 211, Stonington, Conn.

   2d Prize, Miss Helen L. Brown, Webster Pl., Allston, Mass.

4. — 1st Prize, Miss M. S. Brown, 30 Mt. Pleasant Street, Woburn, Mass.

   2d Prize, Mrs. W. J. Whitford, Box 76, Brookfield, N. Y.

5. — 1st Prize, Mrs. J. M. Hobron, 26 W. 133d Street, N. Y. City.

   2d Prize, Miss Jennie R. Welch, Lawrence, Douglas County, Kansas.

6. — 1st Prize, Miss A. M. Fitz, 58 Olive Street, New Haven, Conn.

   2d Prize, Mrs. John Shaw, Red Oak, Iowa.

7. — 1st Prize, Mrs. Harriet U. Nicklin, 73 Beaver Street, New Castle, Pa.

   2d Prize, Mrs. Henry Krieger, Granada, Prowers Co., Col.

8. — 1st Prize, Mrs. A. W. Stratton, Framingham, Mass.

   2d Prize, Miss Susie E. Pratt, 114 Broad Street, E. Weymouth, Mass.

9. — 1st Prize, Mrs. James E. Burgess, 12 N. Fairchild Street, Madison, Wis.

   2d Prize, Miss Susan H. Mann, Box 1076, Greenfield, Mass.

10. — 1st Prize, Miss Annie E. Converse, So. Worthington, Mass.

    2d Prize, Miss Jennie M. Phipps, Stanton, Mich.

11. — 1st Prize, Mrs. J. H. White, St. Augustine, Fla.

    2d Prize, Miss Julia D. Smith, Box 159, W. Medway, Mass.

12. — 1st Prize, Mrs. Lizzie Anthony, Oroville, Cal.

    2d Prize, Mrs. Charles Cleaver, 3962 Ellis Ave., Chicago, Ill.

Owing to the general excellence of work submitted, the task of making the awards was a most difficult one, a decision being reached in all cases only by the closest comparison and consideration of details. Among other ladies of whose contributions especial mention should be made are: Miss Annie J. Lamphier, Lynn, Mass.; the Misses Pauline and Lissie Lowe, Rutledge, Tenn.; the Misses Emma and Daisy Danvers, Lents, Oregon; Mrs. Hamlin Jones, Campbell Hall, N. Y.; Mrs. D. O. Gilbert, Benkleman, Neb.; Mrs. Emily J. S. Reed, Charlotte, N. C.; Miss Ellen M. Bruce, Tallapoosa, Ga.; Miss Elma I. Locke, Redding, Iowa; Miss Emma McFarland, Martinsburg, Ohio; Mrs. Flora Keefe, Turlock, Cal.; Mrs. C. H. Lawrence, Morris, N. Y.; Miss Kate Watkins, Baltimore, Md.; Lucinda A. Mather, Rushville, N. Y.; Miss Lizzie Mackey, Thompson Orphanage, Charlotte, N. C.; Miss Bertha Weaber, Vineland, N. J.; Mrs. H. J. Fleury, Newport News, Va.; Mrs. Anna P. Clark, Colmar, Pa.; Mrs. A. J. Sumner, E. Middlebury, Vt.; Mrs. H. Rosenthal, New York, N. Y.; Miss Carrie S. Marsh, Hallstead, Pa.; Mrs. E. T. Lake, Central City, Col.; Mrs. K. W. Lant, Newton, Iowa; Mrs. Walter L. Eckels, Mechanicsburg, Pa.; Miss Agnes Harbison, Box 29, Goliad, Texas; Miss Carrie H. Beckley, Forestville, Conn.; Miss Jennie de R., South Berwick, Me.; Mrs. Belle S. Grimes, Delavan, Wis.; Alice M. Robinson, Gloucester, Mass.; and Mrs. W. E. Draper, West Roxbury, Mass. Mention should also be made of the large and beautiful varieties of work shown by Mrs. James E. Burgess, Madison, Wis., and others.

MRS. INEZ REDDING,
MRS. O. W. CLAPP,
MISS MATTIE BARRON,
MRS. M. M. HINES,
MRS. A. C. STODDARD.

BOSTON, Nov. 19, 1891.

Our thanks are due the Committee for the judicious manner in which their work has been performed, and to the ladies throughout the country for the interest evinced in this pleasant competition, which will be continued in BARBOUR'S PRIZE SERIES, No. 2, to be issued about Jan. 1, 1892.

Respectfully,

THE BARBOUR BROTHERS COMPANY.

INTRODUCTION.

It is with pardonable gratification that we present "No. 2" of "Barbour's Prize Series," feeling sure it will prove indeed a "prize" to all who delight in lace-making, embroidery, and the great variety of needle-work into which the flax threads so effectively enter. Made up as it is of practical contributions from ladies, North, East, South, and West, it must — apart from the interest given it by the very liberal premium offers — be a welcome and valued addition to works of a similar kind which have preceded it. All directions have been carefully tested, and are so explicitly written that we think no difficulty can be experienced in following them ; many contributors have, however, expressed a willingness to render any assistance that may be desired in working the designs furnished by each, respectively, as the editor herself is always glad to do.

Our "No 1" was an experiment ; that it has proved so successful is due in greatest measure to the warm seconding of our efforts by the ladies of America. For this we thank them ; and also for the many sensible suggestions received, not a few of which will be acted upon in future. Such ideas are always gladly received by the Barbour Brothers Company, who, having the largest and best-equipped linen-thread manufactories in the world, are abundantly able and willing to provide for every want in this line.

A little information regarding the Irish Flax Threads will doubtless be of interest to many. The Barbour Brothers Co., as is well known, have the oldest linen-thread manufactories in the world, their establishment dating from 1784 ; they are also the most extensive, the works at Paterson, N. J., Lisburn, Ireland, and Ottenson, Germany, employing, collectively, five thousand hands, — as many as any two other linen-thread firms in the world. Branch offices, twenty in number, situated in the most important cities of Europe

and America, aid in the distribution of this important product to
every department of trade in which linen threads are used.   To this
firm of thread-makers, for more than one hundred and eight years,
have been awarded the highest honors by the juries of the Interna-
tional Exhibitions, held during the past forty years, principally at
London in 1862, Vienna in 1873, Philadelphia in 1876, Berlin in
1877, Paris in 1878, where also, in addition to the gold medal, they
were awarded "the Grand Prize of Honor of the Linen Section of
Great Britain for distinguished excellence in linen threads and yarns
of all kinds."   This was the only grand prize given to Ireland, and the
only one received by any thread manufacturers in the world.   Also at
the seventeenth exhibition of the Massachusetts Charitable Mechanic
Association, held in Boston, in 1890, they were awarded a gold
medal for "superior excellence in strength and finish of their threads."
It will be seen by this record that the generations of Barbour, as they
succeed each other, have by their close attention to details in their
business kept in touch with the demands of the numerous trades
which use their product, and have earned for their threads a position
of honor and high standard unexcelled by any other.

The superexcellence of the Irish Flax Threads for knitting, crocheting, and all lace work has long been known to ladies everywhere ;
but the introduction of Flax Embroidery Threads is comparatively of
recent date.   The manufacture of the flax fibre into threads sufficiently smooth and flexible for embroidery, and which should receive
perfectly fast dyes satisfactorily, was attended with much difficulty,
only four or five colors being apparently possible at first.   These
difficulties the Barbour Brothers Co., by dint of much costly experi-
menting, were the first to overcome, and to-day the Flax Embroidery
Threads, in an almost unlimited variety of colors, including the newest art shades, cannot be distinguished in point of smoothness, soft-
ness, and color from the best silk.   It is made in three sizes (o, oo,
and S), the latter of sufficient fineness to be used successfully on the
thinnest silk or finest satin, while the coarsest serve admirably for
heavy outlining and other open embroidery stitches, being far superior to filoselle for all purposes to which the latter is adapted.   Often,

when a piece of work is elaborate or closely covered, expense becomes a matter of much importance, and, in any case, one cannot
resist wishing for something less costly than the pure, spun silk.   As
a substitute for the latter, the Flax Embroidery Threads are far
ahead of any material yet introduced, being as perfect and sound in
their way as the purest silk ; and, now that we have them in such
lovely colors and superior quality, the linens are often chosen in
preference to the silk threads, — the pure grades of which are not
always, or frequently, to be had.

CLASSIFICATION OF PRIZES.

Department No. 1.
Crocheted, knitted, and Maltese (or hairpin) laces.

1 Prize,	. .	$50.
4 Prizes of $25 each,		100.
10 "	$10 "	100.
10 "	$5 "	50.
25 Prizes.		$300. **$300.**

Department No. 2. Articles in crocheted or hairpin work, other than lace, for useful or ornamental purposes, such as tidies, lambrequins, curtains, drapes, bedspreads, dress-yokes and sleeves, lamp-shades, purses, collars, cuffs, etc.

1 Prize,	. .	$50.
4 Prizes of $25 each,		100.
10 "	$10 "	100.
10 "	$5 "	50.
25 Prizes.		$300. **$300.**

Department No. 3. Articles in knitted work, other than lace, as noted in department No. 2, with fancy stockings, mitts, infants' bonnets, night-dress cases, etc.

1 Prize,	. .	$50.
4 Prizes of $25 each,		100.
10 "	$10 "	100.
10 "	$5 "	50.
25 Prizes.		$300. **$300.**

Department No. 4. Articles in tatted work of all kinds, lace, cushion covers, passementerie, etc.

1 Prize,	. .	$50.
4 Prizes of $25 each,		100.
10 "	$10 "	100.
10 "	$50 "	50.
25 Prizes.		$300. **$300.**

Department No. 5. Articles in plain and fancy netting, netted guipure, and bobbin work.

1 Prize,	. .	$50.
4 Prizes of $25 each,		100.
10 "	$10 "	100.
10 "	$5 "	50.
25 Prizes.		$300. **$300.**

Department No. 6. Articles in Italian, gobelin, flat, cross-stitch, and similar embroidery, including darned net.

1 Prize,	. .	$50.
4 Prizes of $25 each,		100.
10 "	$10 "	100.
10 "	$5 "	50.
25 Prizes.		$300. **$300.**

Department No. 7. Articles in Kensington, Mountmellick, and outline embroidery, such as bedspreads, doilies, lunch-cloths, centre-pieces, table-scarfs, etc.

1 Prize,	. .	$50.
4 Prizes of $25 each,		100.
10 "	$10 "	100.
10 "	$5 "	50.
25 Prizes.		$300. **$300.**

Department No. 8. Articles in drawn work, Mexican work, and cut work, or Roman embroidery.

1 Prize,	. .	$50.
4 Prizes of $25 each,		100.
10 "	$10 "	100.
10 "	$5 "	50.
25 Prizes.		$300. **$300.**

Department No. 9. Articles in English point, Venetian, Russian, Limoges, or braid work.

1 Prize,	. .	$50.
4 Prizes of $25 each,		100.
10 "	$10 "	100.
10 "	$5 "	50.
25 Prizes.		$300. **$300.**

Department No. 10. Articles of any description, other than specially noted, in which the Irish flax threads are used.

1 Prize,	. .	$50.
4 Prizes of $25 each,		100.
10 "	$10 "	100.
10 "	$5 "	50.
25 Prizes.		$300. **$300.**

250 Prizes.   **$3,000.**

RULES.

ALL articles submitted in competition for the prizes offered must consist of sample or samples of work, with complete directions carefully written out. Samples of knitted, crocheted, and tatted laces, with other work of similar class, should be made from the directions after the latter are written, thus ensuring correctness.

All work must be done with Barbour's Irish Flax Threads, and every description should state exactly what number and size of thread was used, with size of needles employed, if knitted or crocheted work, also the quantity of material needed for tidies, bonnets, bedspreads, etc.

Competitors are not confined to one sample or one department; as many prizes may be competed for as desired. No one person may win more than two prizes, however, one of these being in Department No. 10. It will also be necessary that the competitor state in which department she wishes to enter her work, there frequently being several varieties of needle-work in a single article; a bureau-scarf, for example, may be of linen scrim, decorated with a drawn-work border, outline embroidery, and finished with crochet lace. This competition is not designed for professional needle-workers, but for our friends in all parts of the country, and all will have equal chances of winning. It being understood that *all directions must be absolutely correct*, errors in MSS. will be remedied, if necessary; and new and good ideas will count for more than proper punctuation or correct spelling.

We wish again to suggest that articles on the more difficult or less common needle-work, such as noted in Departments 5, 7, 8, and 9, may perhaps have a greater chance of winning than those on crocheted and knitted laces, for the reason that the competition is reasonably sure to be larger in the latter class. Original work will receive especial attention.   All articles intended for competition must reach the branch office of the Barbour Brothers Company, 67 Lincoln Street, Boston, Mass., on or before February 1, 1893, at which time the competition will close, and prizes will be awarded as soon thereafter as possible.   A committee of ladies to award the prizes will be selected by the Barbour Brothers Company as in the case of the first competition.

Please do not delay in sending work, but make it ready as soon as possible, in order that it may be nicely and properly classified, without haste.   All articles which win prizes will be retained for the Exhibit of Irish Flax Threads at the World's Fair, and, later, the Mechanics' Fair, after which they will be carefully returned to prize-winners.   If articles are designed for sale, we shall be pleased to have prices placed upon them.

Contributions winning 1st and 2d prizes, with such others as may be selected, will be printed in No. 3 of Barbour's Prize Series.   Information concerning needed materials for work, netting-needles, tatting-shuttles, etc., will be gladly furnished those desiring it ; and we trust that our friends everywhere will manifest a cordial appreciation of the generosity of the Barbour Brothers Company by making this prize competition a most spirited one.

MARY E. BRADFORD.

Roxbury, Mass.

EGLANTINE LACE.

FIRST PRIZE ARTICLE.

[Contributed by Miss CARRIE V. WILDEY, Brooklyn, N.Y.]

Materials : Barbour's flax thread, 3-cord, 200-yards spools, No. 80 ; steel hook, size o.

Make a ch of 28 sts, turn.

1. Shell of 6 tc in 3d st of ch, ch 3, 1 dc in 6th st of ch, ch 6, 1 dc in 12th st, ch 6, 1 dc in 18th st, ch 6, 1 dc in 24th st, ch 3, sh in 28th st, turn.

2. Ch 3, sh in sh, ch 5, 1 dc under 6 ch following, ch 6, fasten under 6 ch, ch 5, sh in sh, 1 tc in last st of sh, turn.

3. Ch 3, sh in sh, ch 3, fasten under 5 ch, ch 6, fasten under 6 ch ; now, to form rosette, make 8 tc in dc, 1 dc under 6 ch, 2 tc in same st as 8 tc were made in, by putting hook down through the hole and up through the mesh to the left, 5 more tc in same place, passing hook up through next mesh, 2 tc in same hole, passing hook up through next mesh, join to 1st of the tc with 1 sc, forming a circle of 17 tc ; now, work around the circle, thus : 5 tc through top of next st, 1 dc in next, continue this until you have 9 scallops around circle ; join with 1 dc. Now make 1 dc where ch joins back of rosette, ch 6, fasten under 5 ch, ch 3, sh in sh, 1 tc in last st of sh, turn.

4. Ch 3, * sh in sh, ch 5, under 6 ch, ch 6, under next 6 ch, ch 6, under next ch, ch 5, sh in sh, 1 tc in last st, turn.

5. Ch 3, sh in sh, ch 3, under 5 ch, ch 6, under next ch, ch 6, under next ch, ch 6, under next ch, ch 3, sh in sh, 1 tc in last st, * turn.

6. Like 4th row.

7. Like 5th row.

8. Like 4th row.

9. Ch 3, sh in sh, ch 3, under 5 ch, ch 6, under next ch ; then make the 2d rosette in dc, as before, fasten where ch joins back of rosette, ch 6, fasten in next ch joining rosette, ch 6, fasten under 5 ch, ch 3, sh in sh, 1 tc in last st of sh. To form scallop, ch 5, skip

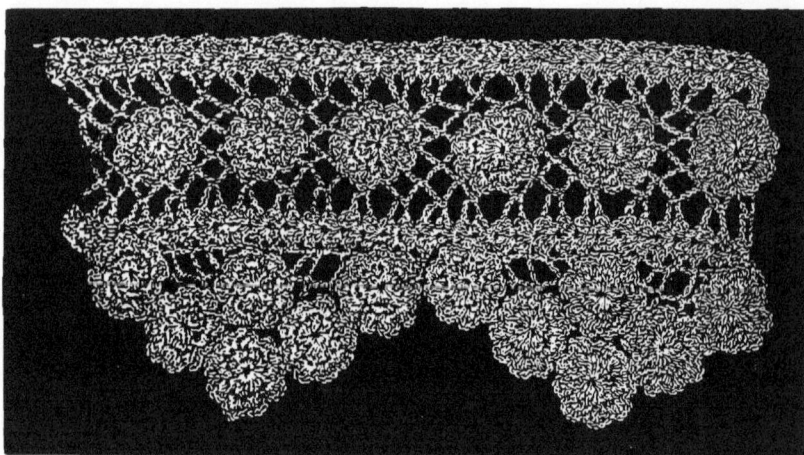

Eglantine Lace.

tc just made, and fasten under next row down side of insertion ; dc under next row, turn.

10. Ch 6, fasten under 5 ch, ch 6, tc in tc, finish like 4th row from *.

11. Like 5th row to * ; then ch 6, fasten under 6 ch of scallop, 6, fasten under next 6 ch, ch 6, fasten under tc, dc under next turn.

12. Ch 6, fasten under 6 ch of scallop, ch 6, fasten under next 6 ch, under next ch, ch 6, tc in tc, finish like 4th row from *.

13. Like 5th row to *, then ch 6, under 6 ch of scallop, ch 6, ch 6, rosette in dc, fasten where ch joins back of rosette,

ch 7, fasten on back of rosette, ch 6, under 6 ch, ch 6, under tc, dc under tc, turn.

14. Ch 6, under 6 ch, ch 6, under next 6 ch, ch 7, under next ch, ch 7, under same chain, ch 7, under next ch, ch 6, under next ch, ch 6, tc in tc, finish like 4th row from *.

15. Like 9th row to scallop; then ch 6, fasten under 6 ch of scallop, ch 6, under next 6 ch, ch 6, under 7 ch, ch 7, under 7 ch, ch 7, under same ch, ch 7, under next ch, ch 6, under next ch, ch 6, under next ch, ch 6, under tc, dc under next tc, turn.

16. Ch 6, fasten under 6 ch, ch 6, under next ch, ch 6, under next ch, ch 6, under 7 ch, ch 7, under 7 ch, ch 7, under next 7 ch, ch 6, under next ch, ch 6, under next ch, ch 6, under next ch, ch 6, tc in tc; finish like 4th row from *.

17. Like 5th row to *; ch 6, under 6 ch of scallop, * rosette in dc, fasten back of rosette, ch 6, fasten back of rosette, ch 6, under next ch, repeat from * until the 5 rosettes are made, fasten last 6 ch in tc at end of 1st row, turn.

Work back with a row of ch sts caught in back of rosettes; finish like 4th row.   Repeat.

The insertion is made by simply leaving off the scallop.

MOUNTAIN ANTIQUE LACE AND INSERTION.

SECOND PRIZE ARTICLE.

[Contributed by Mrs. CHARLES GOFF, Middlebury, Vt.]

Materials : No. 70, 3-cord, 200-yards spools, Barbour's flax thread, ecru or white, and a fine steel hook.

Ch 84, turn.

1. Sh of 3 tc, 2 ch and 3 tc in 4th st of ch, 1 dc in 3d following st, * draw out the st on hook to 1-4 inch, take up thread, draw through this loop, put hook under thread just drawn through and make 1 dc on the thread ; this forms a " knot-stitch;" repeat from * once, pass 5 sts of ch, 1 dc in next st, pass 2, sh in next st, pass 2,

1 tc in next st, ch 2, pass 2, 4 tc in next 4, ch 5, pass 4, 5 dc in next 5, ch 5, pass 4, 4 tc in next 4, ch 2, pass 2, 1 tc in next, pass 2, sh in next, pass 2, 1 dc in next, a double knot-stitch as before directed, pass 5, 1 dc in next, pass 2, sh in next, pass 2, 1 tc in next, ch 2, pass 2, 4 tc in next 4, ch 5, pass 4, 5 dc in next 5, ch 5, pass 4, 4 tc in next 4, ch 10, turn.

2. 4 tc in last 3 sts of 10 ch and 1st tc of last row, ch 2, miss 2, 4 tc, ch 5, 3 dc in middle 3 of 5 dc, ch 5, 4 tc (on last 3 of 5 ch and 1st tc following), ch 2, pass 2, 1 tc in next, ch 2, tc in next tc, sh in sh, make 1 knot-stitch, 1 dc before the knot in last row (under 2 loops), 1 dc after knot, another knot-stitch, sh in sh, tc in tc, ch 2, tc in tc, ch 2, miss 2, 4 tc, ch 5, 3 dc in 5 dc, ch 5, 4 tc, ch 2, 1 tc in last of 4 tc of last row, ch 2, 1 tc in next tc, sh in sh, 1 knot-stitch, fasten with 1 dc before and after knot of last row, 1 knot-stitch, sh in sh, tc in loop of 3 ch at end of sh, turn

3. Ch 3, sh in sh, 1 dc in end of sh of last row, double knot-stitch, 1 dc in 1st st of 2d sh, sh in sh, tc in next tc, ch 2, tc in next tc, ch 2, tc in next tc, ch 2, 4 tc in last of 4 tc of preceding row and 1st sts of 5 ch, ch 3, 1 dtc (thread over twice) in middle of 3 dc, ch 3, 4 tc, 3 sp (each formed by 2 ch, pass 2, and 1 tc in next), sh in sh, fasten down as before, 1 double knot-stitch, fasten to 1st st of next sh, sh in sh, tc in next tc, 3 sp, 4 tc, ch 3, 1 dtc in middle of 3 dc, ch 3, 4 tc, ch 3, 1 dtc under 2 ch, ch 3, miss 3 tc, 4 tc in last tc and under ch following, turn.

4. Ch 10, 4 tc (as in 2d row), ch 5, 3 dc in last of 3 ch, over dtc, and in 1st of 3 ch following, ch 5, 4 tc, ch 2, 4 tc, 4 sp, sh in sh, single knot-stitch, fasten, single knot-stitch, sh in sh, tc in next tc, 4 sp, 4 tc under 3 ch, ch 2, 4 tc under next 3 ch, 4 sp, sh in sh, after last tc, single knot-stitch, fasten, single knot-stitch, sh in sh, tc in 3 ch at end, turn.

5. Ch 3, sh in sh, fasten with 1 dc in last tc of previous sh, double knot-stitch, fasten with 1 dc in 1st st of next sh, sh in sh, tc in next tc, 5 sp, 4 tc, 5 sp, sh in sh after last tc, fasten, double knot-stitch, fasten, sh in sh, tc in next tc, 5 sp, 4 tc, ch 5, 5 dc over 3 dc and 1 st on each side, ch 5, 4 tc, turn.

6. Ch 10, 4 tc, ch 5, 3 dc, ch 5, 4 tc, ch 2, 4 tc, 4 sp, sh in sh, after last tc, 1 single knot-stitch, fasten as before, with 1 dc on each side of centre knot of preceding row, 1 single knot-stitch, sh in sh, tc in tc, 4 sp, 4 tc, 1 sp, 4 tc, 4 sp, sh in sh, after last tc, single

Mountain Antique Lace and Insertion.

knot-stitch, fasten, single knot-stitch, fasten, sh in sh, 1 tc in ch 3 at end of row, turn.

7. Ch 3, sh in sh, 1 dc in last st of sh, double knot-stitch, 1 dc in 1st st of next sh, sh in sh, tc in tc, 3 sp, 4 tc, ch 3, 1 dtc under 2 ch, ch 3, 4 tc, 3 sp, sh in sh after last tc, fasten, double knot-stitch,

fasten in next sh, sh in sh, 1 tc in next tc, 3 sp, 4 tc, ch 3, 1 dtc under 2 ch, ch 3, 4 tc, ch 3, 1 dtc in middle of 3 dc, ch 3, 4 tc, ch 3, 1 dtc under 2 ch, ch 3, 4 tc, turn.

8. Ch 10, 4 tc, ch 5, 3 dc, ch 5, 4 tc, ch 2, 4 tc, ch 5, 3 dc, ch 5, 4 tc, 2 sp, sh in sh, single knot-stitch, fasten, single knot-stitch, sh in sh, tc in tc, 2 sp, 4 tc, ch 5, 3 dc, ch 5, 4 tc, 2 sp, sh in sh, 1 single knot-stitch, fasten, single knot-stitch, sh in sh, 1 tc in 3 ch, turn.

9. The insertion, or part ending with 4th sh, is from here repeated from 1st row, hence a repetition of directions is not necessary. After the heading, make tc in tc, ch 2, 4 tc, ch 5, 5 dc, ch 5, 4tc, ch 5, 5 dc, ch 5, 4 tc, turn.

10. Ch 10, 4 tc, ch 2, 4 tc, ch 5, 3 dc, ch 5, 4 tc, ch 2, 4 tc, ch 5, 3 dc, ch 5, 4 tc, 2 sp; heading, beginning with sh in sh, after last tc, like 2d row.

11. Heading like 3d row; tc in tc, 3 sp, 4 tc, ch 3, 1 dtc in middle of 3 dc, ch 3, 4 tc, ch 3, 1 dtc under 2 ch, ch 3, 4 tc, ch 3, 1 dtc, ch 3, 4 tc, ch 3, 1 dtc, ch 3, 4 tc, turn.

12. Ch 10, 4 tc, ch 5, 3 dc, ch 5, 4 tc, ch 2, 4 tc, ch 5, 3 dc, ch 5, 4 tc, ch 2, 4 tc, 4 sp; heading like 4th row.

13. Heading like 5th row; tc in tc, 5 sp, 4 tc, ch 5, 5 dc, ch 5, 4 tc, ch 5, 5 dc, ch 5, 4 tc, turn. This completes half of the point, which now begins to diminish.

14. Chain 5, 4 tc, worked after the 4 tc of last row, instead of before them, ch 5, 3 dc, ch 5, 4 tc, ch 2, 4 tc, ch 5, 3 dc, ch 5, 4 tc, ch 2, 4 tc, 4 sp; heading like 6th row.

15. Heading like 7th row; 1 tc in tc, following sh, 3 sp, 4 tc, ch 3, 1 dtc under 2 ch, ch 3, 4 tc, ch 3, 1 dtc, ch 3, 4 tc, ch 3, 1 dtc, ch 3, 4 tc, ch 3, 1 dtc, ch 3, 4 tc, turn.

16. Ch 5, 4 tc, ch 2, 4 tc, ch 5, 3 dc, ch 5, 4 tc, ch 2, 4 tc, ch 5, 3 dc, ch 5, 4 tc, 2 sp; heading like 8th row.

17. Heading like 1st row; tc in tc, 2 sp, 4 tc, ch 5, 5 dc, ch 5, 4 tc, ch 5, 5 dc, ch 5, 4 tc, turn.

18. Ch 5, 4 tc, ch 5, 3 dc, ch 5, 4 tc, ch 2, 4 tc, ch 5, 3 dc, ch 5, 4 tc, 1 sp; heading like 2d row.

19. Heading like 3d row; tc, 3 sp, 4 tc, * ch 3, 1 dtc, ch 3, 4 tc, repeat from * twice, turn.

20. Ch 5, 4 tc, ch 2, 4 tc, ch 5, 3 dc, ch 5, 4 tc, ch 2, 4 tc, 4 sp; heading like 4th row.

21. Heading like 5th row; tc, 5 sp, 4 tc, ch 5, 5 dc, ch 5, 4 tc, turn.

22. Ch 5, 4 tc, ch 5, 3 dc, ch 5, 4 tc, ch 2, 4 tc, 4 sp; heading like 6th row.

23. Heading like 7th row; tc, 3 sp, 4 tc, ch 3, 1 dtc, ch 3, 4 tc, ch 3, 1 dtc, ch 3, 4 tc, turn.

24. Ch 5, 4 tc, ch 2, 4 tc, ch 5, 3 dc, ch 5, 4 tc, 2 sp; heading like 8th row.

Repeat the entire pattern from the 1st row to the length desired.

For the edge, fasten the thread in 1st row after the last cluster of 4 tc, make 10 tc in 1st loop of ch, on the edge; 1 dc between the 2 clusters of 4 tc, and repeat around the point.

ANTIQUE LACE, FOR CURTAINS, ETC.

[Contributed by Mrs. H. ROSENTHAL, New York, N.Y.]

Materials : No. 50 3-cord, 200-yards spools, Barbour's flax thread, and a steel hook.

Ch 75.

1. Miss 3 sts, 6 tc in next 6 sts, * ch 3, 1 dc in 3d st, ch 3, 1 tc in 3d st, repeat from * 3 times, forming 4 sps, 18 tc in next 18 sts, repeat from * to * to form 3 sps, 6 tc in last 6 sts, turn.

2. Ch 3, to take place of 1st tc, 1 tc on each following tc, * ch 5, tc on next tc, * repeat from * to * twice, 18 tc on tc, repeat from * to * 4 times, tc on each following tc.

3. Ch 14, miss 3 sts going back, 12 tc on next 12 sts, * ch 3, miss 2, 1 dc in next st, ch 3, miss 2, 1 tc on next st, * repeat from * to * 3 times, 11 tc on 5 ch and following 6 tc, ch 3, miss 2, 1 dc,

ch 3, miss 2, 7 tc on 7 tc, repeat from * to   3 times, 6 tc on last 6 tc, turn

4. Ch 3, tc on next 6 tc, 3 sp (as the spaces are formed always

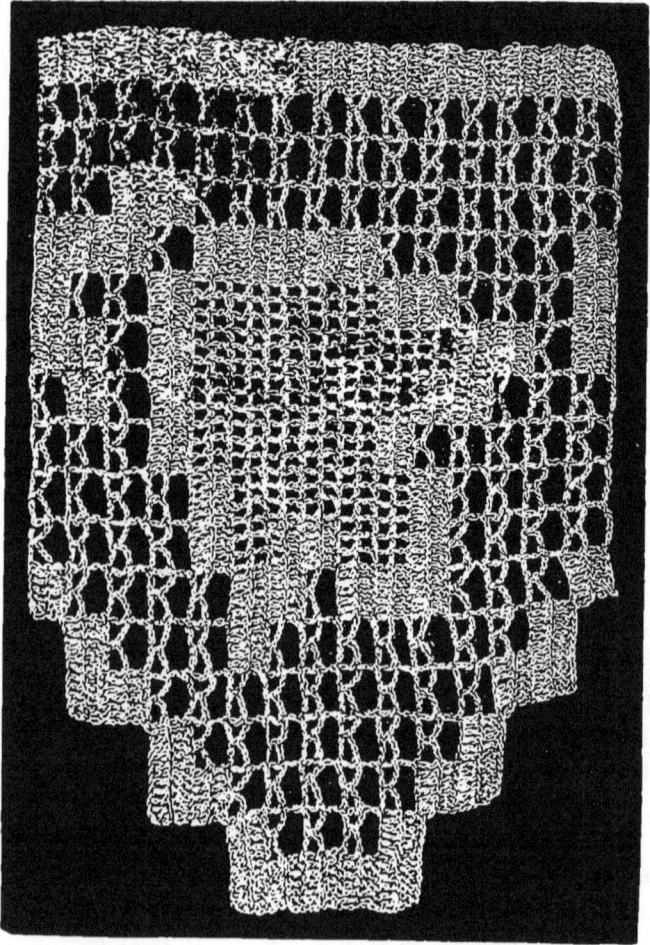

Antique Lace for Curtain.

h   s described, by chs of 3, caught in centre of 5 ch, and by
   separately, there is no need of details hereafter), 7 tc, 1 sp,
      tc, turn.

5. Ch 3, 6 tc, 8 sp, 12 tc, 2 sp, 7 tc in last 7 tc, ch 3, turn.

6. Repeat last row, backward, making ch of 5 over sp.

7. Ch 14, miss 3 going back, 12 tc, 5 sp, 25 tc, 1 sp, 7 tc, 2 sp, 7 tc, ch 3, turn.

8. Repeat last row, making 5 ch over sp, and putting tc on tc.

9. Ch 3, 6 tc, 4 sp, 12 tc, then * ch 1, miss 1, 1 tc in next, repeat 11 times, 6 tc in next 6 sts, 2 sp, 7 tc, ch 3, turn.

10. Like last row, 5 ch over sp, and tc on tc.

11. Ch 14, miss 3 going back, 12 tc, 3 sp, 13 tc, ch 1, 18 tc, each separated by 1 ch, 6 tc on next 6 sts, 3 sp, 7 tc, ch 3, turn.

12. Same as last row, going backward, and making 5 ch over sp, and tc on tc.

13. Ch 3, 6 tc, 5 sp, 13 tc, ch 1, 15 tc, each separated by 1 ch, 6 tc on next 6 tc, 3 sp, 7 tc on last 7 tc, ch 3, turn.

14. Repeat 13th row downward, as before.

15. Ch 3, 6 tc, 6 sp, 7 tc, 15 tc, each separated by 1 ch, then 6 tc, 3 sp, 7 tc, ch 3, turn.

16. Like last row, going back.

17. Ch 3, 6 tc, 5 sp, 7 tc, ch 1, 18 tc, each separated by 1 ch, 6 tc on next 6 tc, 3 sp, 7 tc, ch 3, turn.

18. Like last row, going back; always ch 5 over sp in even rows.

19. Ch 3, 12 tc, 4 sp, 7 tc, ch 1, 6 tc, each separated by 1 ch, 6 tc in next 6 tc, ch 1, 6 tc, each separated by 1 ch, 6 tc in next 6, 4 sp, 7 tc, ch 3, turn.

20. Like last row, going down.

21. Work along 12 tc in sc, 1 in each, ch 3, 6 tc, 3 sp, 19 tc, 1 sp, 7 tc, ch 1, 3 tc, each separated by 1 ch, 6 tc, 4 sp, 7 tc, ch 3, turn.

22. Like last row, going back.

23. Ch 3, 12 tc, 6 sp, 13 tc, 5 sp, 7 tc, ch 3, turn.

24. Like last row, going back.

25. Make 12 sc in 12 tc, ch 3, 6 tc, 6 sp, 7 tc, 5 sp, 7 tc, ch 3, turn.

26. Like last row, going back.

27. Ch 3, 12 tc, 11 sp, 7 tc, ch 3, turn.

28. Like last row, remembering always to ch 5 over each sp in even rows.

The pattern always repeats from 1st to 28th rows, with the exception that 12 sc in 1st 12 tc, at every scallop, followed by 3 ch, precede the 1st 6 tc in 1st row.

INSERTION FOR ANTIQUE LACE.

[Contributed by Mrs. H. ROSENTHAL, New York, N.Y.]

Use No. 50, 3-cord, 200-yards spools Barbour's flax thread, and steel hook of medium size.   Make a ch of 100 sts.

1. Miss 3 of ch, 6 tc, 3 sp (as described in making the lace), 19 tc, counting all, 8 sp, 7 tc, ch 3, turn.

As every alternate or even row is worked directly over and repeats the preceding row, it seems unnecessary to describe these.   Always ch 5 over the sp, putting tc in tc.   The 3 ch at the end of every row takes the place of a tc.   In giving the number of tc, all are counted, including that which forms one side of a sp.

3. 6 tc, 3 sp, 7 tc, 1 sp, 13 tc, 7 sp, 7 tc, ch 3, turn.   Remember always to work down, with 5 ch over sp, making 3 ch at the end.

5. 6 tc, 2 sp, 13 tc, 10 sp, 7 tc, ch 3, turn.

7. 6 tc, 2 sp, 7 tc, 1 sp, 25 tc, 6 sp, 7 tc, ch 3, turn.

9. 6 tc, 3 sp, 7 tc, * ch 1, miss 1, 1 tc in next, repeat from * 10 times, ch 1, 13 tc, 4 sp, 7 tc, ch 3, turn.

11. 6 tc, 3 sp, 7 tc, * ch 1, miss 1, 1 tc in next, repeat 17 times, 12 tc, 2 sp, 7 tc, ch 3, turn.

13. 6 tc, 3 sp, 7 tc, * ch 1, miss 1, 1 tc in next, repeat 14 times, 12 tc, 3 sp, 7 tc, ch 3, turn.

15. 6 tc, 3 sp, 7 tc, * ch 1, miss 1, 1 tc in next, repeat 14 times, 6 tc, 4 sp, 7 tc, ch 3, turn.

17. 6 tc, 3 sp, 7 tc, * ch 1, miss 1, 1 tc in next, repeat 17 times, 6 tc, 3 sp, 7 tc, ch 3, turn.

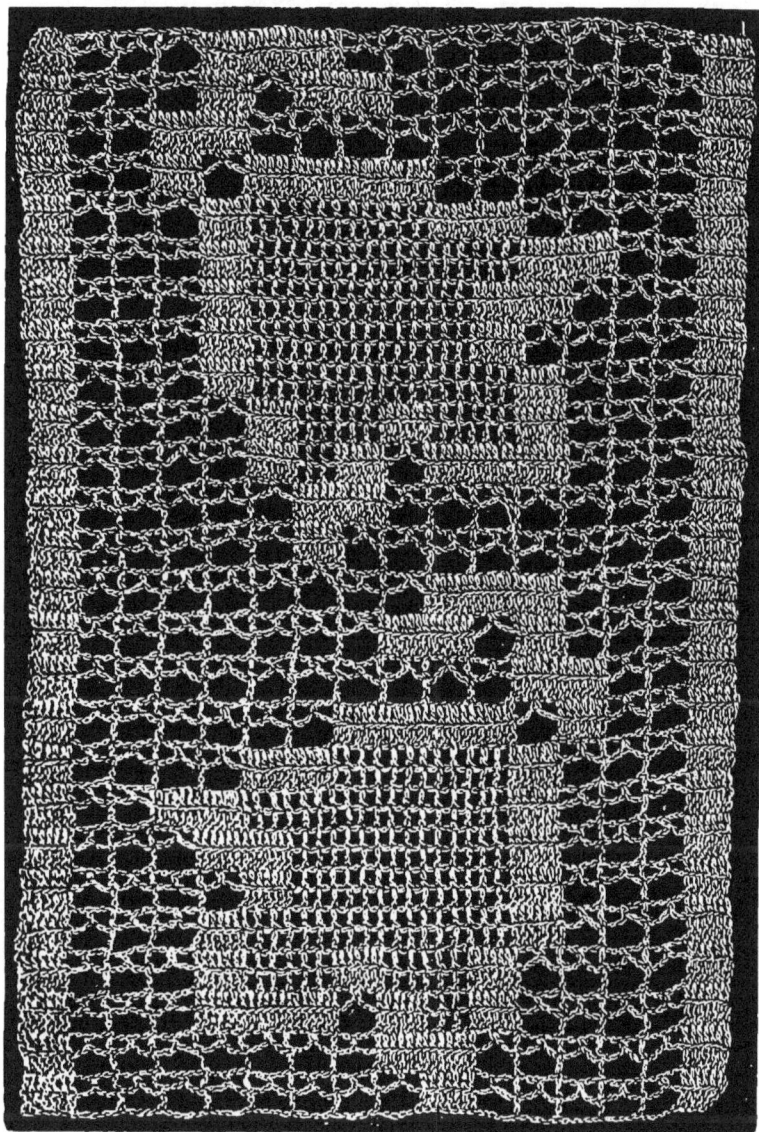

Insertion for Antique Lace.

19. 6 tc, 4 sp, 7 tc, * ch 1, miss 1, 1 tc in next, repeat 5 times, 6 tc, * ch 1, miss 1, 1 tc in next, repeat 5 times, 6 tc, 3 sp, 7 tc, ch 3, turn.

21. 6 tc, 4 sp, 7 tc, * ch 1, miss 1, 1 tc in next, repeat twice, 6 tc, 1 sp, 19 tc, 3 sp, 7 tc, ch 3, turn.

23. 6 tc, 5 sp, 13 tc, 7 sp, 7 tc, ch 3, turn.

25. 6 tc, 5 sp, 7 tc, 8 sp, 7 tc, ch 3, turn.

27. 6 tc, 8 sp, 19 tc, 3 sp, 7 tc, ch 3, turn.

29. 6 tc, 7 sp, 13 tc, 1 sp, 7 tc, 3 sp, 7 tc, ch 3, turn.

31. 6 tc, 10 sp, 13 tc, 2 sp, 7 tc, ch 3, turn.

33. 6 tc, 6 sp, 25 tc, 1 sp, 7 tc, 2 sp, 7 tc, ch 3, turn.

35. 6 tc, 4 sp, 13 tc, * ch 1, miss 1, 1 tc in next, repeat 11 times, 6 tc, 3 sp, 7 tc, ch 3, turn.

37. 6 tc, 2 sp, 13 tc, * ch 1, miss 1, 1 tc in next, repeat 17 times, 6 tc, 3 sp, 7 tc, ch 3, turn.

39. 6 tc, 3 sp, 13 tc, * ch 1, miss 1, 1 tc in next, repeat 14 times, 6 tc, 3 sp, 7 tc, ch 3, turn.

41. 6 tc, 4 sp, 7 tc, * ch 1, miss 1, 1 tc in next, repeat 14 times, 6 tc, 3 sp, 7 tc, ch 3, turn.

43. 6 tc, 3 sp, 7 tc, * ch 1, miss 1, 1 tc in next, repeat 17 times, 6 tc, 3 sp, 7 tc, ch 3, turn.

45. 6 tc, 3 sp, 7 tc, * ch 1, miss 1, 1 tc in next, repeat 5 times, 6 tc, ch 1, miss 1, 1 tc in next, repeat 5 times, 6 tc, 4 sp, 7 tc, ch 3, turn.

47. 6 tc, 3 sp, 19 tc, 1 sp, 7 tc, * ch 1, miss 1, 1 tc in next, repeat twice, 6 tc, 4 sp, 7 tc, ch 3, turn.

49. 6 tc, 7 sp, 13 tc, 5 sp, 7 tc, ch 3, turn.

51. 6 tc, 8 sp, 7 tc, 5 sp, 7 tc, ch 3, turn.

Work back, the 52d row, and repeat from 1st row.

PICOT POINT LACE.

[Contributed by Miss EMMA McFARLAND, Martinsburg, Ohio.]

Materials: Barbour's flax thread, No. 80, 3-cord, 200-yards spools, and a steel hook, No. 2.

Ch 31 sts, turn.

1. Sh of 3 tc, 1 ch and 3 tc in 4th st of ch, 1 dc in 8th st, draw out st on hook 1-4 inch, take up thread and draw through this loop, put hook under thread just drawn through, between it and the long st, take up thread, draw through, then take up thread and draw through both sts now on hook. This makes 1 knot-stitch. Make another in the same way, 1 dc in 13th st of ch, ch 3, 1 dtc (thread over twice) in same st, working off only 1st 2 loops, leaving 2 on hook, 1 dtc in same stitch, working off 2 loops and leaving 3 on hook. Draw through all these at once; make 2 dtc in the 18th st of ch (working off 2 loops only, in same way), then draw through the 3 sts and draw through the stitch on hook, ch 3, 1 dc in same st of ch, 2 knot-stitches as before, 1 dc in 23d st of ch, sh in 27th st, 1 dc in last st, ch 6, turn.

2. Sh in sh, 1 knot-stitch, 1 dc in centre of 2 knot-stitches of last row, 1 knot-stitch, 2 dtc as before in centre st of the dtc sts of last row, ch 3, 1 dc in same st, ch 3, 2 dtc in same st, 1 knot-stitch, 1 dc in centre knot of last row, 1 knot-stitch, sh in sh, * ch 7, 1 sc in top of 1st sh made, turn.

3. Under the 7 ch make 3 dc, 1 picot (a picot consisting of ch 3, put hook down through the top and out front of last dc made, under 2 threads, take up thread, draw through the 2 threads and st on hook), 4 dc, ch 6, turn, 1 sc in top of last dc made, turn, under 6 ch work 3 dc, 1 p, * 5 dc, 1 p, 3 dc; under last half of 7 ch work 3 dc, 1 p, 3 dc, * sh in sh, 1 dc in last st of sh in last row, 2 knot-stitches, 1 dc in st at end of 1st cluster of dtc in last row, ch 3, 2 dtc in same st (always working off as described in previous rows), 2 dtc in st at end of 2d cluster, ch 3, 1 dc in same st, 2 knot-stitches, 1 dc in 1st st of next sh, sh in sh, 1 dc in last st of sh, ch 6, turn.

4. Like 2d row to * : ch 7, 1 sc between 2 sh on edge, turn ; repeat from * to * in 3d row, 3 dc, ch 7, turn, 1 sc in the centre of the 5 dc in top f loop in last row, turn.

5. Repeat from * to * in 3d row, 5 dc, 1 p, 3 dc ; under last

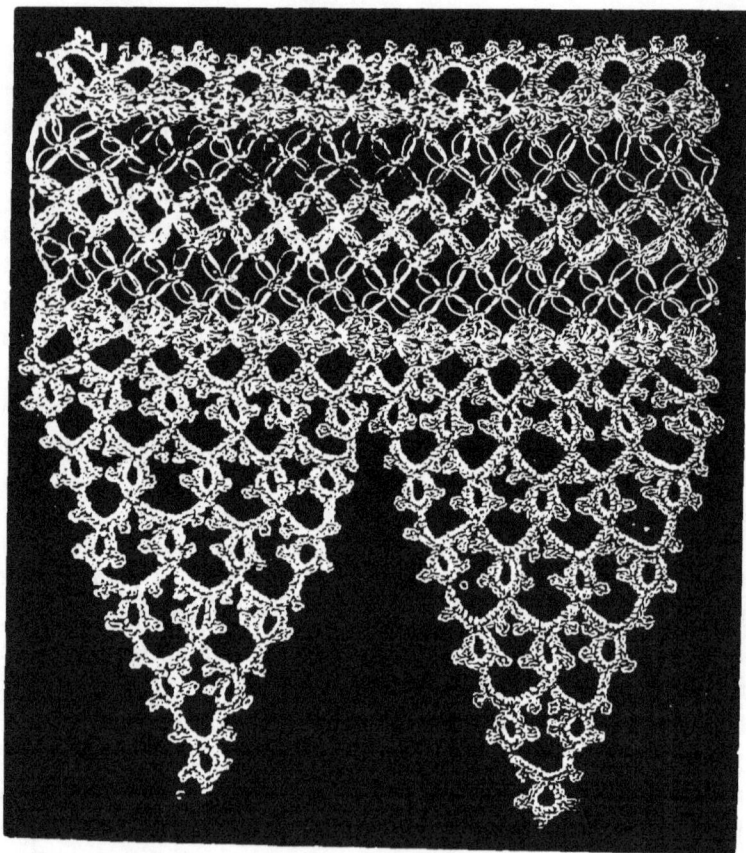

P   P   L

3 dc, and same under last half of next
from 3d *.

ch 7, 1 sc between next 2 sh on edge,
in 3d row, 3 dc, ch 7, turn, 1 sc in centre

of 5 dc in top of 1st loop in last row, turn, repeat from * to * in 3d row, 3 dc, ch 7, 1 dc in centre of 5 dc in top of 2d loop in last row, turn.

7. Repeat from * to * in 3d row, 5 dc, 1 p, 3 dc; under last half of each 7 and 6 ch work 3 dc, 1 p, 3 dc; finish like 3d row from *.

Continue to work in this way until the point is as deep as desired. In the loop at the point make 3 picots. Finish loops at top of pattern with 3 dc, 1 p, 3 dc, 1 p, 3 dc, 1 p, 3 dc. For the insertion make both edges alike.

PERI LACE.

[Contributed by Miss IDA F. WILDEY, Brooklyn, N.Y.]

Materials: Barbour's flax thread, No. 80, 3-cord, 200-yards spools, fine steel hook. No. 0 is a good size.

Ch 36 sts, turn.

1. Make group of 3 loops by working 1 tc in 5th st, ch 3, tc in same st, ch 3, tc in same st, ch 4, tc in next 3d st, ch 3, tc in next 3d st, ch 4, tc in next 3d st, group of 3 loops, as before, by working 3 more tc separated by 3 ch in same st, ch 4, tc in next 4th st, ch 3, tc in next 4th st, ch 4, tc in next 4th st, group of 3 loops, ch 4, tc in next 3d st, ch 3, tc in next 3d st, ch 4, tc in next 3d st, group of 2 loops in same st, ch 4, turn.

2. Group of 3 loops under 2d 3 ch of 2 loops, ch 3, tc over 3 ch, ch 4, tc in 1st loop of group of 3 loops, ch 3, repeat as before to form group of 3 loops, and the same in 2d and 3d loop of previous group, ch 3, tc in 3 ch, ch 4, group of 3 loops in each loop of next group, ch 4, tc in 4 ch, ch 3, tc in middle loop of next group, group of 2 loops in same loop, ch 4, turn.

3. Group of 3 loops in 2d loop, ch 4, tc in 3 ch, ch 3, tc in 2d loop of large group following, ch 4, tc in 5th loop, group of 3 loops in same, ch 4, tc in 8th loop of same large group, ch 3, tc in 3 ch, ch 3, tc in 2d loop of next group of 9, ch 3, group of 3 loops in 5th

loop, ch 4, tc in 8th loop, ch 3, tc in 3 ch, ch 4, group of 2 loops in middle loop of group following, chain 4, turn.

4. Group of 3 loops in 2d loop, ch 3, tc in 3 ch, ch 4, 3 groups of 3 loops each in 1st, 2d, and 3d following loops, ch 3, tc in 3 ch, ch 4, 3 groups of 3 loops each in next 3 loops, ch 4, tc in 3 ch, ch 3, group of 2 loops in middle of 3 loops following, ch 4, turn.

5. Like 3d row.

6. Like 4th row.

Repeat these 2 rows. At the end of the 9th row begins the scallop. Ch 14, fasten with sc at end of 9th row, in same st in which it began, but on lower side, ch 3, fasten in same loop with sc, ch 1, turn.

10. Make 1 tc in 14 ch, ch 1, repeat 13 times, fasten in 1st loop of group of 2 loops; finish like 4th row.

11. Like 3d row to scallop; ch 1, tc over 1 ch, between first and 2d tc of preceding row, ch 1, tc over next 1 ch, repeat until 6 tc are made, ch 3, tc in same ch as last tc, ch 1, tc in next 1 ch, proceed until 6 more tc are made, fasten with 1 sc in 4 ch between 2 groups of loops, ch 3, fasten in next 4 ch between groups, ch 3, turn.

12. Tc in loop between 1st and 2d tc, ch 3, tc in next ch, repeat 5 times, ch 4, tc in same ch as last, ch 3, tc in next ch, repeat 6 times, fasten last 3 ch with 1 sc in 4 ch between next 2 groups of loops, finish like 4th row.

13. Like 3d row to scallop; ch 3, fasten in 4 ch on edge, ch 3, group of 3 loops (4 tc, each separated by 3 ch) between 1st and 2d tc, ch 1, miss 3 ch, group of 3 in next 3 ch, ch 1, miss 3 ch, group of 3 in next, ch 3, miss 3 ch, group of 3 loops in next, ch 3, miss 3, group of 3 in next, ch 1, miss 3 ch, group of 3 in next, ch 1, miss 3, group of 3 in next 3 ch, ch 3, fasten in 4 ch between groups of loops on the edge, ch 3, turn.

14. Fasten in 1st loop of group of 2, ch 2, group of 3 loops in middle loop of group of 3, ch 3, group of 3 loops in middle loop of next group, ch 3, same in next, ch 4, same in next, ch 4, same in next, ch 3, same in next, ch 3, same in next, ch 2, fasten in 3 ch connecting 2 groups of loops, ch 4, finish like 4th row.

15. Like 3d row to scallop ; ch 3, fasten in 4 ch connecting 2 groups of loops, ch 1, miss 1st loop, groups of 3 in 2d and 3d loops, fasten in 3 ch, 3 groups of 3 loops each in next 3 loops, fasten in ch between, repeat until you have 7 large groups, missing also the 3d loop of 7th small group, ch 1, fasten in 4 ch connecting 2 groups, ch 2, fasten in 1st loop of group of 2, ch 3, turn.

16. Tc in middle loop of 1st group of 3, ch 4, tc in middle loop

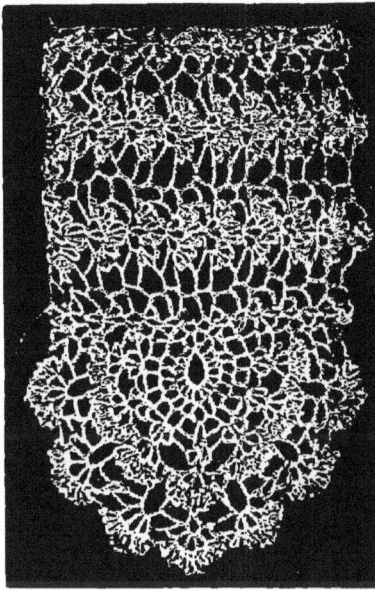

Peri Lace.

of 2d group, * ch 4, tc in middle loop of next group of 3, repeat to top of scallop, where ch 3, 1 tc in same loop as last tc, then ch 4, and proceed as on other side, ch 3, fasten in 4 ch between groups, ch 4, finish like 4th row.

17. Like 3d row to scallop ; chain 3, fasten under 4 ch between groups, ch 3, tc in 3 ch, ch 3, tc in 4 ch, ch 3, group of 3 in next 4 ch, ch 3, tc in next 4 ch, ch 3, tc in next 4 ch, ch 4, group of 3 loops in next 4 ch, ch 4, tc in next 4 ch, ch 3, tc in next 4 ch, ch 4,

3 loops in ch of 4, ch 4, tc in 4 ch, ch 3, group of 3 loops in next loop, ch 3, tc in next 4 ch, ch 4, and proceed until there are 7 groups of 3 loops each, ch 4, tc in 4 ch, ch 3, tc in next ch, ch 1, fasten with sc in middle loop of group of 3, ch 3, fasten back in next loop, turn.

18. Ch 3, 1 tc in 3 ch, ch 3, 1 tc in 4 ch, ch 3, * group of 3 loops in each of 3 loops following, ch 3, repeat from * around scallop, ch 3, 1 tc in 4 ch, ch 3, fasten in 4 ch connecting groups of loops.

Repeat to the length desired.

For heading, fasten in thread, * ch 4, 1 sc in 4 ch between groups, repeat.

NORWEGIAN INSERTION.

[Contributed by Mrs. C. H. GOFF, Middlebury, Vt.]

Materials : No. 50, Barbour's flax thread, white, 3-cord, 200-yards spools, and fine steel hook.

Ch 64, turn.

1. 1 dc in 5th st, * ch 5, pass 4, 1 dc in next, repeat from * 11 times, ch 3, turn.

2. Dc in centre of 5 ch, sh of 5 tc in next dc, fasten in centre of 5 ch, sh in next dc, fasten in centre of next 5 ch, * ch 5, fasten in centre of next 5 ch, repeat from * 7 times, shell in next dc, fasten in centre of 5 ch, shell in next dc, fasten in loop at end, ch 5, turn.

3. Fasten in centre of 1st sh, ch 5, fasten in centre of next sh, * ch 5, fasten in centre of 5 ch, repeat from * once, * shell in next fastening dc, fasten in centre of 5 ch, repeat once from last *, ch 5, fasten in 5 ch, sh in next dc, fasten in 5 ch, sh in next dc, fasten in 5 ch, ch 5, fasten in next 5 ch, * ch 5, fasten in centre of sh, repeat from * once, ch 5, fasten in loop at the end, ch 3, turn.

4. Fasten in centre of 5 ch, * sh in next dc, fasten in 5 ch, repeat once, ch 5, fasten in 5 ch, ch 5, fasten in centre of next sh, sh in next dc, fasten in centre of next sh, sh in next dc, fasten in 5 ch, * sh in next dc, fasten in centre of next sh, repeat once from *, * ch

5, fasten in 5 ch, repeat once, sh in next dc, fasten in 5 ch, sh in next dc, fasten in loop at the end, ch 5, turn.

5. Like 3d row.

6. Like 4th row.

7. Fasten in centre of sh, ch 5, fasten in next sh, * ch 5, fasten in centre of next 5 ch, repeat 10 times, putting the fastening dc in centre of 5 ch or of sh, as the case may be, the last in loop at end ; ch 3, turn.

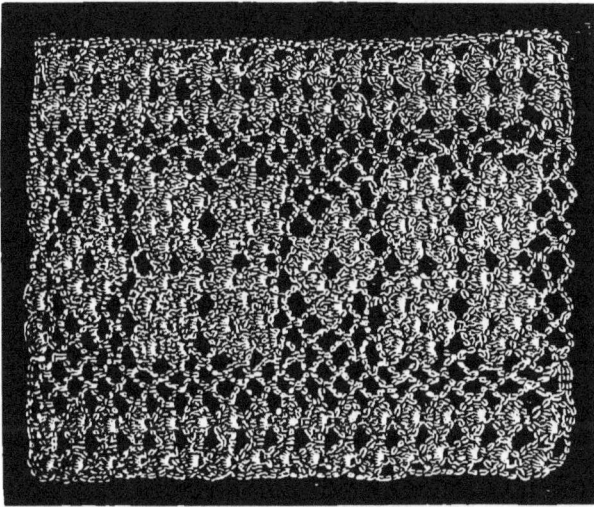

Norwegian Insertion.

8. Fasten in 5 ch, sh in dc, fasten in 5 ch, sh in dc, fasten in 5 ch, * ch 5, fasten in next 5 ch, repeat once, * sh in next dc, fasten in 5 ch, repeat 3 times, * ch 5, fasten in 5 ch, repeat once, sh in next dc, fasten in 5 ch, sh in next dc, fasten in 5 ch at end, ch 5, turn.

9. Fasten in sh, ch 5, fasten in sh, * ch 5, fasten in 5 ch, repeat once, * sh in dc, fasten in centre of next sh, sh in next dc, fasten in sh, ch 5, fasten in centre of sh, repeat from * once, putting last dc in centre of 5 ch, * ch 5, fasten in 5 ch, repeat twice, ch 5, fasten in loop at end, ch 3, turn.

10. Like 8th row.

11. Like 9th row.

12. Fasten in 5 ch, * sh in dc, fasten in 5 ch, repeat once, * ch 5, fasten in 5 ch, repeat 7 times, * sh in dc, fasten in 5 ch, repeat once, ch 5, turn.

13. Fasten in sh, ch 5, fasten in sh, * ch 5, fasten in 5 ch, repeat 3 times, sh in next dc, fasten in 5 ch, * ch 5, fasten in 5 ch, repeat 5 times, ch 3, turn.

14. Fasten in 5 ch, * sh in dc, fasten in 5 ch, repeat once, * ch 5, fasten in 5 ch, repeat twice, sh in dc, fasten in next sh, sh in dc, fasten in 5 ch, * ch 5, fasten in 5 ch, repeat twice, * sh in dc, fasten in 5 ch, repeat once, ch 5, turn.

15. Fasten in sh, ch 5, fasten in sh, * ch 5, fasten in 5 ch, repeat twice, sh in dc, fasten in next sh, ch 5, fasten in sh, sh in dc, fasten in 5 ch, * ch 5, fasten in 5 ch, repeat 4 times, ch 3, turn.

16. Fasten in 5 ch, * sh in dc, fasten in 5 ch, repeat once, * ch 5, fasten in 5 ch, repeat once, ch 5, fasten in sh, sh in dc, fasten in 5 ch, sh in dc, fasten in next sh, * ch 5, fasten in 5 ch, repeat twice, * sh in dc, fasten in 5 ch, repeat once, ch 5, turn.

17. Fasten in sh, ch 5, fasten in sh, * ch 5, fasten in 5 ch, repeat twice, ch 5, fasten in sh, sh in dc, fasten in sh, * ch 5, fasten in 5 ch, repeat 5 times, ch 3, turn.

Repeat from 2d row.

This is very easily worked if one remembers that the fastening dc always comes in the centre of 5 ch or of sh. A lace to match is readily made by omitting the double row of shells on one edge and adding a shell point.

UNIQUE LACE.

[Contributed by Miss ANNIE J. LAMPHIER, Lynn, Mass.]

This lace is made in hairpin work and crochet. Use No. 70, 3-cord, 200-yards spools, Barbour's flax thread, a very fine crochet-hook, and a common steel hairpin. If preferred, the hairpin work may be made of coarser linen than the rest.

Make the strips of hairpin work (single) as long as desired, having the number of loops on each side divisible by 18. Make a 4th strip for the scallops, making 41 sts in this strip to every 18 sts in the other strips, and 1 more.

Unique Lace.

1. Take a short strip of hairpin work, make 3 tc in 1st 2 loops, taken together, 3 tc in next 2 loops; repeat to end of row, and cut the thread.

2. Repeat 1st row on opposite side of strip, beginning at the end where 1st row left off, turn.

3. Ch 5, 1 dc in 5th tc, ch 5, 1 dc between 3d and 4th groups of tc ; repeat to end of row, cut thread.

4. Take another short strip of hairpin work, make 1 tc in 1st 2 loops (taken together), ch 3, 1 tc in same place, * miss 1 loop, 1 tc in next 2, ch 3, 1 tc in same place ; repeat from * to end of row, turn.

5. 7 tc under 3 ch, 1 dc between 2 tc ; repeat, turn.

6. Ch 5, * dc in next dc, ch 5 ; repeat from *, turn.

7. To join the strips of insertion, take the strip first made : 1 dc in 3d st of 1st 5 ch, ch 2, dc in 3d st of 5 ch in 2d strip, * ch 2, dc in 3d st of next 5 ch of 1st strip, ch 2, dc in 3d st of next 5 ch of 2d strip ; repeat from * to end, ch 5, fasten in 1st strip, cut thread. Care must be taken in joining to have both strips right side out.

8. Take work wrong side out and repeat 4th row on opposite side of 2d strip.

9. Like 5th row.

10. Like 6th row, omitting last 5 ch, cut thread.

11. Take longest strip for scallops, sc in 1st loop, ch 3, * sc in next loop, ch 5, (3 tc in next 2 loops ch 2, miss 1 loop) 4 times, 1 tc in next 2 loops, ch 2, miss 1 loop, (1 tc in next 2 loops, ch 1, miss 1 loop) twice, (1 tc in next 2 loops, ch 2, miss 1 loop) twice, (3 tc in next 2 loops, ch 2, miss 1 loop) 3 times, 3 tc in next 2 loops, ch 5, (sc in next loop, ch 3) twice ; repeat from *, turn.

12. Sc in next loop (over sc of last row), ch 7, 3 tc under 5 ch, (ch 1, 3 tc under next 2 ch) 3 times, (ch 1, 1 tc under 2 ch) twice, (1 tc under next 1 ch) twice, (1 tc under next 2 ch, ch 1) twice, (3 tc under next 2 ch, ch 1) 3 times, 3 tc under next 2 ch, ch 7, (sc in loop over next sc of last row, ch 3) twice, sc in loop over next sc of last row, ch 5, sc in last st of 5 ch of last row, ch 6, 1 tc under same 5 ch of last row, (ch 3, 1 tc under next 2 ch) 4 times, ch 1, 1 tc under each of next 4 chs, ch 1, 1 tc under next 2 ch, (ch 3, 1 tc under next 2 ch) 3 times, ch 3, 1 tc under 5 ch, ch 3, sc in 1st st of same 5 ch, ch 5, (sc in next loop, over sc of last row, ch 3) twice ; repeat, turn.   If desired, the scallops may be made all alike instead of alternating the solid and open-work centres.

13. Dc in next loop, over sc of last row, ch 5, dc in next sc, ch 7, 2 dtc in 1st 3 ch, 4 dtc in next 3 ch, (4 tc in next 3 ch) twice, 1 tc in next 3 ch, drawing thread through but once and keeping last 2 loops on hook, 2 more tc in same place, retaining last loop of each, thus giving 4 loops on hook, thread over, draw through all, 1 tc in each of next 5 holes, retaining top loops, as before, draw through the 6 loops, sc in top of last cluster of 3 tc, (2 tc in next 3 ch, sc in opposite cluster of 4 tc, 2 tc in same place) twice, 2 dtc in next 3 ch, sc in opposite cluster of 4 dtc, 2 dtc in same place, 1 dtc in next 3 ch, sc in opposite dtc, dtc in same place, sc in 7 ch, ch 7, dc in sc of last row, ch 5, dc in loop over sc of last row, (ch 3, dc in next loop over sc of last row) twice, ch 5, dc in 4th st of 5 ch of last row, (ch 7, dc in next 1 ch) twice, (ch 5, dc in next 1 ch) 3 times, ch 3, pass over 6 tc, dc in next 1 ch, ch 2, dc in last 5 ch, ch 2, dc in next 2 ch, (ch 2, dc in opposite 5 ch, ch 2, dc in next 1 ch) twice, ch 3, dc in opposite 7 ch, ch 3, dc in 7 ch of last row, ch 3, dc in opposite 7 ch, ch 3, dc in 2d st of 7 ch of last row, ch 5, (dc in loop over sc of last row, ch 3) twice ; repeat and cut the thread. These directions are for an even number of scallops, alternating patterns.

14. Take last short strip of hairpin work, miss 1st 3 sts, dc in next 3 loops, taken together, * ch 3, miss 2 loops, shell of 8 tc in next 2 loops, ch 3, miss 2 loops, dc in next 3 loops ; repeat from *, ch 2, turn.

15. 1 tc between 1st 2 tc of last row, (ch 1, 1 tc between next 2 tc) 6 times, ch 2, dc in dc of last row, ch 2 ; repeat from *, turn.

16. 1 tc in dc of last row, 3 tc under 1 ch, (3 tc under next 1 ch) 5 times, repeat ; 1 tc in dc of last row, ch 7, turn.

17. Dc between 3d and 4th clusters of tc, ch 7, dc in single tc between fans, ch 7, repeat, fastening last 7 ch with 1 dc over tc, ch 3, turn.

18. To join 3d strip to other 2, dc in 4th st of 7 ch, ch 3, take piece already done, dc in dc of 10th row (being careful to see that both pieces are right side out), * ch 3, dc in 4th st of 7 ch of last row, ch 3, dc in 3d st of 2d 5 ch, ch 3, dc in 4th st of 7 ch, ch 3,

dc in 2d dc of 10th row (counting ahead) ; repeat from *, cut thread.

19. Like 14th row, on opposite side of strip, making the 8 tc opposite the dc of 14th row.

20. Like 15th row.

21. Like 16th row.

22. Like 17th row, omitting 3 ch.

23. To join the scallops to the rest, ch 7, take scallops, * 1 dc in 1st dc of scallop, ch 3, dc in 4th st of 7 ch of last row, ch 3, dc in 3d st of 5 ch, ch 3, dc in 4th st of 7 ch of last row, ch 3, dc in dc in middle of top of scallop, ch 3, dc in 4th of 7 ch, ch 3, dc in 3d st of 5 ch, ch 3, dc in 4th of 7 ch, ch 3, dc in 2d dc, ch 3, dc in 4th of 7 ch, ch 3, dc in next dc, ch 3, dc in 4th of 7 ch, ch 3, dc in dc in middle of scallop, ch 3, dc in 4th of 7 ch, ch 3, dc in next dc, ch 3, dc in 4th st of 7 ch, ch 3 ; repeat from * and cut thread. The threads should be neatly fastened at back of work.

This is an original pattern, and considered very pretty. It is capable of many changes and adaptations. The scallops may be attached to either insertion, taken alone, thus making a narrower lace. In coarse linen, or macramé, the scallops may be added to the 2d insertion to make an edge for small table.

To make the hairpin work, take the hairpin in left hand, prongs up, keeping the hook, with loop of thread on it, in right hand. Hold thread at back of hairpin as in crocheting, bring hook around outside of left prong from the back, and put between the prongs ; draw thread through loop on hook, pass thread between prongs toward front and round right prong to back, draw through loop on hook, and make 1 dc in loop on left prong ; * turn hairpin from right to left, holding thread as in crocheting, draw thread through loop on hook, dc in loop on left prong ; repeat from * to desired length. Take out hairpin when full, replacing last 2 or 3 loops.

LANGTRY LACE.

FIRST PRIZE ARTICLE.

[Contributed by Mrs. H. W. HOWLAND, Xenia, Ill.]

Materials : Barbour's flax thread, No. 80, 3-cord, 200-yards spools, and 2 knitting-needles, No. 19.

Cast on 56 sts ; knit across plain.

1. K 4, o, p 2 tog, o, p 2 tog, k 2, o, k 3, sl, n and b, k 3, o, k 1, o, k 3, sl, n and b, k 3, o, k 1, o, k 3, sl, n and b, k 3, o, k 2, o, p 2 tog, o, p 2 tog, k 2, o 2, n, k 1, (o, p 2 tog) 3 times.

2. (O, p 2 tog) 3 times, k 3, p 1, k 2, o, p 2 tog, o, p 2 tog, k 33, o, p 2 tog, o, p 2 tog, k 4.

3. K 4, (o, p 2 tog) twice, k 3, o, k 2, sl, n and b, k 2, o, k 3, o, k 2, sl, n and b, k 2, o, k 3, o, k 2, sl, n and b, k 2, o, k 3, (o, p 2 tog) twice, k 6, (o, p 2 tog) 3 times.

4. (O, p 2 tog) 3 times, k 6, (o, p 2 tog) twice, k 33, (o, p 2 tog) twice, k 4.

5. K 4, (o, p 2 tog) twice, k 4, o, k 1, sl, n and b, k 1, o, k 5, o, k 1, sl, n and b, k 1, o, k 5, o, k 1, sl, n and b, k 1, o, k 4, (o, p 2 tog) twice, k 2, o 2, n, o 2, n, (o, p 2 tog) 3 times.

6. (O, p 2 tog) 3 times, k 2, p 1, k 2, p 1, k 2, (o, p 2 tog) twice, k 33, (o, p 2 tog) twice, k 4.

7. K 4, (o, p 2 tog) twice, k 5, o, sl, n and b, o, k 7, o, sl, n and b, o, k 7, o, sl, n and b, o, k 5, (o, p 2 tog) twice, k 8, (o, p 2 tog) 3 times.

8. (O, p 2 tog) 3 times, k 8, (o, p 2 tog) twice, k 33, (o, p 2 tog) twice, k 4.

K 4, (o, p 2 tog) twice, k 4, n, o, k 1, o, k 3, sl, n and b, k

9. k 1, o, p 2 tog and b, k 3, o, k 1, o, n, k 4, o, p 2 tog)
twice, k 2, o, n, o, n, o, n, o, p 2 tog 3 times.

10. o, p 2 tog 3 times, k 2, p 1, 3 times, k 2, o, p 2
tog twice k 11, o, p 2 tog twice, k 4.

11. K, o, p 2 tog twice, k 2, n, o, k 3, o, k 2, sl, n and b, k
2, o, n, o, k 2, sl, n and b, k 2, o, k 3, o, n, k 3, o, p 2 tog twice,
k 11, o, p 2 tog 2 times.

12. o, p 2 tog 3 times, k 11, o, p 2 tog twice, k 33, o, p
2 tog 2 times k 4.

13. K 4, o, p 2
tog twice, k 2, n, o, k
3, o, k 1, sl, n and b, k
1, o, k 3, o, k 1, sl, n
and b, k 1, o, k 3, o, n,
k 2, o, p 2 tog, twice,
k 2, o, o, n, 4 times,
k 1, o, p 2 tog 3
times.

14. o, p 2 tog, 3
times, k 3, p 1, k 2 4
times, o, p 2 tog
twice, k 33, o, p 2
tog twice, k 4.

15. K 4, o, p 2
tog twice, k 1, n, o,
k 3, o, sl, n and b,
twice, o, k 3, o, n, k 1
o, p 2 tog twice, k
15, o, p 2 tog 3
times.

16. o, p 2 tog ... knitting with knitting needle lift 12 sts
.... k 1 .... o p 2 tog twice, k

.... stitch, simply k 4
... lighten at the top.

DOUBLE-SHELL LACE.

SECOND PRIZE ARTICLE.

[Contributed by Mrs. MELISSA MITCHELL, Russelville, E. Tennessee.]

Materials: Barbour's flax thread, No. 100, 3-cord, 200-yards spools, 2 steel needles, No. 18.

Cast on 44 sts; knit across plain.

1. Sl 1, k 2, o 2, n, k 7, o, n, o, n, o, n, k 6, o 2, n, k 7, o 2, n, k 7, o, p 2 tog.

2. O, p 2 tog, k 9, p 1, k 9, p 1, k 21, p 1, k 5.

3. Sl 1, k 2, o 2, n, o 2, n, k 7, o, n, o, n, o, n, k 5, o 2, n, o 2, n, k 6, o 2, n, o 2, n, k 6, o, p 2 tog.

4. O, p 2 tog, k 8, p 1, k 2, p 1, k 8, p 1, k 2, p 1, k 20, p 2, k 2, p 1, k 3.

5. Sl 1, k 2, o 2, n, o 2, n, o 2, n, k 8, p, n, o, n, o, n, k 4, * o 2, n, o 2, n, o 2, n, k 6, repeat from *, o, p 2 tog.

6. O, p 2 tog, * k 8, p 1, k 2, p 1, k 2, p 1, repeat from *, k 20, p 1, k 2, p 1, k 2, p 1, k 5.

7. Sl 1, k 11, take last st back on left-hand needle, draw next 6 sts over, replace st, k 5, o, n, o, n, o, n, k 12, take back last st, draw 6 over, replace st, k 10, take back last st, bind over 7, instead of 6, replace st.

8. O, p 1, k 42.

9. Sl 1, k 2, o 2, n, k 11, o, n, o, n, o, n, k 2, o 2, n, k 7, o 2, n, k 7, o, p 2 tog.

10. Like 2d row.

11. Sl 1, k 2, o 2, n, o 2, n, k 11, o, n, o, n, o, n, k 1, * o 2, n, o 2, n, k 6, repeat from *, o, p 2 tog.

12. Like 4th row.

13. Sl 1, k 2, o 2, n, o 2, n, o 2, n, k 11, o, sl and b 5 times, k 1, * o 2, n, o 2, n, o 2, n, k 6, repeat from *, o, p 2 tog.

14. Like 6th row.

15. Sl 1, k 11, take last st back, draw 6 over, replace st, k 4, (o, sl and b) 3 times, k 11, take last st back, draw 6 over, replace st, k 10, take back last st, draw 7 over, and replace st.

16. Like 8th row.

17. Sl 1, k 2, o 2, n, k 10, (o, sl and b) 3 times, k 3, o 2, n, k 7, o, 2, n, k 7, o, p 2 tog.

18. Like 2d row.

19. Sl 1, k 2, o 2, n, o 2, n, k 8, (o, sl and b) 3 times, k 4, o 2, n, o 2, n, k 6, o 2, n, o 2, n, k 6, o, p 2 tog.

20. Like 4th row.

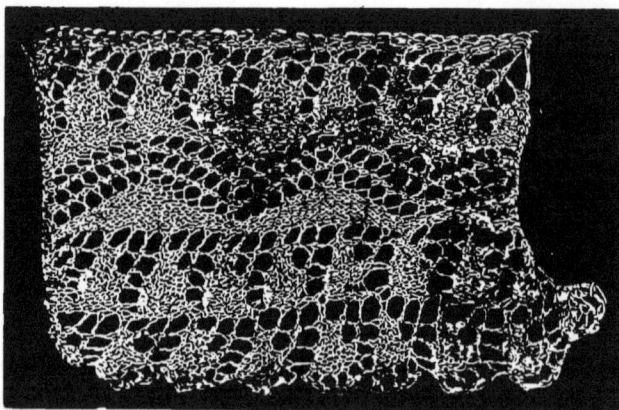

21. Sl 1, k 2, o 2, n, o 2, n, o 2, n, k 7, (o, sl and b) 3 times, k 5, * o 2, n, o 2, n, o 2, n, k 6, repeat from *, o, p 2 tog.

22. Like 6th row.

23. Sl 1, k 11, take last back st, draw over 6, replace st, (o, sl and b) 3 times, k 15, take last st back, draw 6 over, replace st, k 10, take last st back, draw 7 over, replace st.

24. Like 8th row.

Repeat from 1st row. It will be understood that, in forming the ll, the sts drawn over are allowed to fall between the needles, over which they are slipped being then knitted back upon the than l needle before proceeding.

TORCHON LACE.

[Contributed by Mrs. HAMLIN JONES, Campbell Hall, N.Y.]

Materials : Barbour's flax thread, No. 100, 3-cord, 200-yards spools, and 2 steel needles, No. 17.

Cast on 19 sts ; knit once across plain.

1. Sl 1, k 8, * p 2 tog, leave thread forward, k 1, repeat from * twice, o, k 1.

2. O 2, sl and b 1 (that is, sl 1, k 1, pass sl st over), k 9, p 9.

3. Sl 1, k 7, * p 2 tog, leave thread forward, k 1, repeat twice from *, o, k 1, o, n, and drop last loop ; this makes the picot edge.

4. O 2, sl and b 1, o, sl and b 1, k 9, p 8.

5. Sl 1, k 6, * p 2 tog, leave thread forward, k 1, repeat twice from *, o, k 1, o, n, o, n, drop last loop.

6. O 2, sl and b 1, o, sl and b 1, o, sl and b 1, k 9, p 7.

7. Sl 1, k 5, * p 2 tog, leave thread forward, k 1, repeat twice from *, o, k 1, o, n, o, n, o, n, drop last loop.

8. O 2, sl and b 1, * o, sl and b 1, repeat from * twice, k 9, p 6.

9. Sl 1, k 4, p 2 tog, leave thread forward, k 1, repeat twice from *, o, k 1, o, n, o, n, o, n, o, n, drop last loop.

10. O 2, sl and b 1, * o, sl and b 1, repeat from * 3 times, k 9, p 5.

11. Sl 1, k 3, * p 2 tog, leave thread forward, k 1, repeat twice from *, o, k 1, o, n, o, n, o, n, o, n, o, n, drop last loop.

12. O 2, sl and b 1, * o, sl and b, repeat 4 times from *, k 9, p 4.

13. Sl 1, k 2, * p 2 tog, leave thread forward, knit 1, repeat twice from *, o, k 1, o, n, o, n, o, n, o, n, o, n, drop last loop.

14. O 2, sl and b 1, * o, sl and b 1, repeat from * 5 times, k 9, p 3.

15. Sl 1, k 1, * p 2 tog, leave thread forward, k 1, repeat twice from *, o, k 1, o, n, o, n, o, n, o, n, o, n, o, n, drop last loop.

16. O 2, sl and b, *o, sl and b, repeat 6 times from *, k 9, p 2.

17. Sl 1, k 3, * o, p 2 tog, k 1, repeat from *, o, k 3 tog, n, o, n, o, n, o, n, o, n, o, n, o, n, drop last loop.

18. O 2, sl and b 1, * o, sl and b 1, repeat 5 times from *, k 7, p 4.

19. Sl 1, k 4, * o, p 2 tog, k 1, repeat from *, o, n, n, o, n, o, n, o, n, o, n, o, n, drop last loop.

20. O 2, sl and b, * o, sl and b, repeat 4 times from *, k 7, p 5.

21. Sl 1, k 5, * o, p 2 tog, k 1, repeat from *, o, n, n, o, n, o, n, o, n, o, n, drop last loop.

22. O 2, sl and b, * o, sl and b, repeat 3 times from *, k 7, p 6.

23. Sl 1, k 6, * o, p 2 tog, k 1, repeat from *, o, n, n, o, n, o, n, o, n, drop last loop.

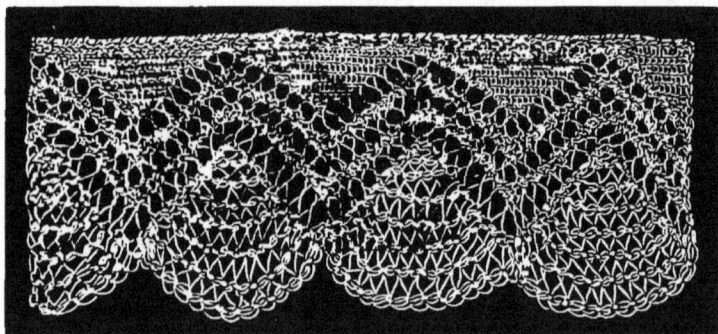

Torchon Lace.

24. O 2, sl and b, * o, sl and b, repeat 2 times from *, k 7, p 7.

25. Sl 1, k 7, * o, p 2 tog, k 1, repeat from *, o, n, n, o, n, o, n, drop last loop.

26. O 2, sl and b, * o, sl and b, repeat from *, k 7, p 8.

27. Sl 1, k 8, * o, p 2 tog, k 1, repeat from *, o, n, n, o, n, drop last loop.

28. O 2, sl and b, o, sl and b, k 7, p 9.

29. Sl 1, k 9, * o, p 2 tog, k 1, repeat from *, o, n, n, drop last loop.

30. O 2, sl and b, k 7, p 10.

Repeat from 1st row. Though seemingly tedious in detailing, this lace may be knitted very rapidly and without much thought. It is odd and very lace-like.

LEAF TIDY.

FIRST PRIZE ARTICLE.

[Contributed by Miss ALICE HINCKLEY, Stonington, Conn.]

Materials : Barbour's flax thread, No. 50, 3-cord, 200-yards spools, and fine steel hook.

Beginning with the small wheel, which is surrounded by 8 pointed leaves, ch 6, join.

Fig. 1.

1. Ch 3, to take place of 1 tc, 15 tc in ring, join to top of 3 ch with 1 sc.

2. Ch 6, miss 2 and make 1 tc between next 2 tc, * ch 3, miss 2, 1 tc between next, repeat 6 times, forming 8 sps, in all, ch 3, join to 3d of 6 ch with 1 sc.

3. Ch 3, for 1 tc, 2 tc in 1st sp, ch 7, 3 tc in same sp, * 3 tc in

Fig. 2.

last sp, ch 7, 3 tc in same sp, repeat from * 6 times, making 8 sps of 7 ch, and join with 1 sc to top of 3 ch at beginning.

1 4 tc under loop of 7 ch, 1 dc between following groups of each; repeat from * all around, and fasten the thread neatly.

This forms the centre. Make 8 leaves to join the 8 scallops as follows:

1. Ch 14, turn; miss 2, 1 dc in each of 11 following, and 3 dc in last st, 10 dc down other side of ch, ch 1, turn. The 24 sts are held throughout in making the leaf, which is begun, as will be observed, at the point or centre. Widening by putting 3 sts in 1 makes up for the sts dropped to form the serrate edge.

2. Miss the ch st and 1st dc, 10 dc in next 10 sts, 3 in centre of 3 widening dc of last row, and 11 dc in next 11 sts, down other side, ch 1, turn.

3. Miss 1 ch and 1st dc, 11 dc in next 11 sts, 3 dc in top, 10 dc in 10 dc down other side, ch 1, turn.

Continue in this way, alternating 10 and 11 dc, with the 3 dc always in the same st at top, until there are 6 ridges on the wrong side and 5½ on the right. Always work in the back loop of the st, as described in the ribbed table-mats on page 43 of "Barbour's Prize Series,

Fig. 3.

No. 1." Both sides of the leaf will thus be alike, with the exception that the 6th rib is not completed on the right side. In the last row, make the 1st of the 3 sts at the top, 1 sc in the middle of scallop of 14 tc of centre, then 2 dc in same place as 1st dc, and complete the row. Make another leaf, as before, join to the preceding at the beginning of last row, omitting the 1 ch, joining to the next scallop of small wheel at the top of leaf, as directed. The 8th leaf is joined at the end of last row to the 1st leaf, in same manner.

A tidy of medium size requires 3 rows of these figures (illustrated in detail by Fig. 1), 3 in a row. They are joined at the tips of the leaves, by 2's, with needle and thread — the same of which the tidy is made or a little finer. Fig. 2 shows a section of the tidy with the

8-leaved figures joined, the spaces being filled by wheels (Fig. 3) worked as follows :

Ch 6, join.

1. Ch 3, for 1st tc, 15 tc in ring, join to top of 3 ch with 1 sc.

2. Ch 6, * miss 2, 1 tc between next 2, ch 3, repeat from * until 8 sps are formed, join to 3d of 6 ch.

3. Ch 3, 5 tc in 1st sp, * tc on tc, 5 tc in next sp, repeat from * all around, join to top of 3 ch.

4. Ch 6, * miss 3, 1 tc between next 2, ch 3, repeat to form 1·· sps, fasten last 3 ch to 3d of 6 ch.

5. Ch 3 for 1st tc, 2 tc in 1st sp, ch 7, 3 tc in same sp, * 3 tc in next sp, ch 7, 3 tc in same sp, repeat to form 16 loops of 7 ch, join to top of 3 ch.

6. 14 tc in loop of 7 ch, 1 dc between groups of 3 tc each following, repeat all around, end with 1 dc, and fasten off.

The wheel may be fastened in the spaces with needle and thread, or joined in when working, between 7th and 8th tc of every 4th scallop, these coming at the joining of the tips of leaves. For a square tidy of 9 8-leaved figures, 4 of these wheels will be required ; for one of 12 figures (4 rows of 3 figures each), 6 wheels will be wanted.

Though very showy, this tidy is simple and rapidly done. The figures may be used in other ways; combined with strips of ribbon crossed to form squares they make another sort of tidy. Other wheels than those described may be used to fill the spaces between figures, if desired.

TOILET SET.

SECOND PRIZE ARTICLE.

[Contributed by Miss HELEN L. BROWN, Allston, Mass.]

Make for the dressing-case, mats, or a scarf, as preferred. These should be made of linen scrim, finished with a two-inch hemstitched hem, and trimmed with crocheted wheel-lace. Draw 4 threads all around, twice the width of the hem from the edge, turn in a very little of the raw edge and baste, to hold it in place nicely, then turn this down to the drawn threads and hem with Barbour's spool linen, No. 100, taking up 4 threads at a time.

Use Barbour's écru flax thread, 3-cord, 200-yards spools, No. 50, and fine steel crochet-needle, for the lace, which is made as follows:

Cushion Cover.

1. Ch 4, join; ch 3 for 1st tc, 19 tc in ring, join to top of 3 ch.

2. Ch 4, 1 tc between next 2 tc, ch 1, repeat all around, putting 1 tc and 1 ch between each tc of preceding round, fasten with sc to 3d of 4 ch.

3. Ch 4, 2 dtc under 1st 1 ch, * ch 3, 3 dtc under next 1 ch, repeat from * all around, ch 3, fasten to top of 4 ch.

4. Ch 4, 1 dc under 3 ch, repeat all around.

This completes 1 wheel. The wheels are joined to each other in the 4th row; make 2 ch, fasten with dc in 4 ch of previous wheel, ch 2, fasten with dc between groups of 3 in the wheel you are making. Repeat until they are connected 4 times, then finish as in first wheel.

After a sufficient number of wheels have been made, crochet around the outer edge; ch 3, 1 picot (consisting of 5 ch caught in a loop with 1 sc in 1st st), ch 3, fasten with 1 dc under next 4 ch; repeat all around.

The cushion cover is made entirely of wheels. There will be spaces between the wheels when joined, which are to be filled thus: Fasten thread in th ch of wheel, ch 3, 1 picot, ch 3, fasten with dc into next space, which is at the junction of two wheels, ch 3, picot, ch 3, fasten in next 4 ch, and so on till the circle is filled. There should be 8 picots. Join, draw thread through, and fasten off neatly.

This is an original design, and very pretty and simple.

PICOT COLLAR.

[Contributed b Mrs. D. H. GILBERT, Benkleman, Neb.]

Materials : Barbour's flax thread, No. 80, 3-cord, 200-yards spools, and a fine steel hook. Make a ch the length desired for collar, turn.

1. Miss 3, 1 tc in every st of ch, turn.

2. Ch 3, 1 tc in each of 15 tc * ch 6, make a picot by fastening back in 5th st of ch from needle with sc, ch 1, miss 2 tc of last row, tc in next 15 tc, repeat from * to end of row, turn.

3. Ch 3, * tc in each tc of last row except 1 next to picot, make 1 picot as before (ch 6, fasten back in 5th st, ch 1), 1 tc in picot of last row, 1 picot, made as described, 1 tc in same place, 1 picot, miss 1st tc, and repeat from * to end of row, turn.

4. Ch 3, * tc in tc except last next to picot, then 1 picot, 1 tc in 1 tc, picot, 1 tc in picot of last row, picot, 1 tc in same, picot, tc on 2d tc of last row, picot, miss 1st tc following, and repeat from * to end of row, turn.

5. Ch 3, * tc in each tc except 1 next to picot, make 1 picot, 1 tc on 1st tc, picot, tc on next tc, picot, tc in picot loop of last row, picot, tc in same loop, make 3 more picots in the same way, miss 1st tc, repeat from * to end of row, turn.

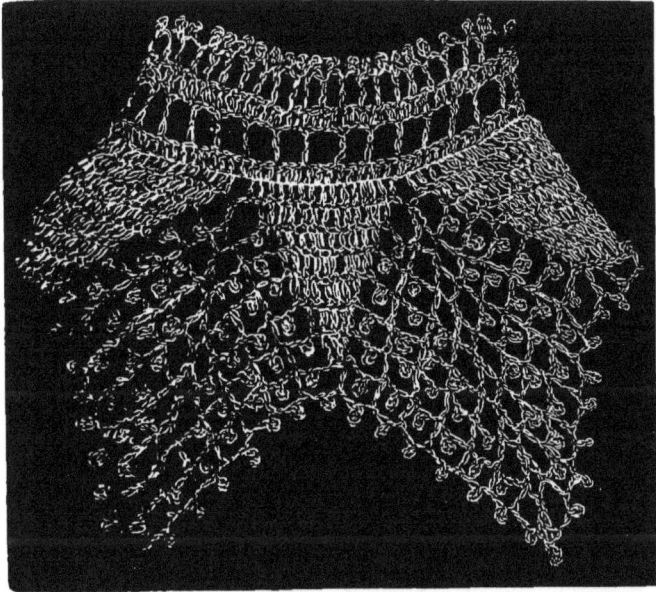

Picot Collar.

Proceed in this way for 4 rows more, the plain point of tc decreasing by 1 tc on each side with every row, and the picot point widening in the same manner as described in the 5th row. It is so simple that explanation seems unnecessary. The 9th row will consist entirely of picots, with 1 tc in centre of plain point. At the end of collar will be a half-point, with straight edge.

Heading :

1. Fasten in top of 1st tc, ch 6, miss 2 sts, 1 dtc in next st, * ch 2, miss 2, 1 dtc in next, repeat from * to the end ; this forms spaces for ribbon.

2. Ch 3, 1 tc in each st of last row.

3. Ch 2, 1 picot, as previously described, miss 2, 1 tc in next st, * picot, miss 2, tc in next, repeat to end of row.

A very pretty "pine-apple" collar is made of the same thread by using the pattern in "Barbour's Prize Series, No. 1," page 26. Make same as pattern there given, using but 1 row of shells for the heading, and fasten but 2 of the scallops together in joining the pine-apples. Make a heading as follows :

1. 1 tc in top of each shell, with 3 ch between each tc, turn.

2. 1 tc under each ch of 3, with 3 ch between each.

3. 9 tc under 1st 3 ch, 1 sc under next 3 ch, repeat to end of row.

INFANT'S BONNET.

[Contributed by Mrs. K. W. LANT, Newton, Ia.]

Materials : Barbour's flax thread, No. 60, 3-cord, 200-yards spools, and a medium-sized steel hook.

1. Ch 7, join. Ch 3, 14 tc in ring, join to top of 3 ch.

2. Widen every st, by putting 2 tc in top of each tc of last row.

3. Widen every 2d st.

4. Widen every 3d st.

Continue in this way, increasing the number of sts between the widenings of each row until, in the 10th row, you widen every 9th st. Each row, it must be remembered, is begun with 3 ch to take place of a tc, and the last tc is joined to the top of 3 ch with 1 sc.

11. Crochet plain (that is, without widening), putting tc in tc, to within 30 sts of the beginning, ch 3, turn. The next 3 rows are worked back and forth over this row, tc in tc, without widening.

15. Turn the work, ch 17, fasten in 3d st from end, * ch 17, fasten in 3d st from last fastening, repeat from * to the end, that is,

over top of bonnet. The 30 sts left at the back are not to be worked over in this way.

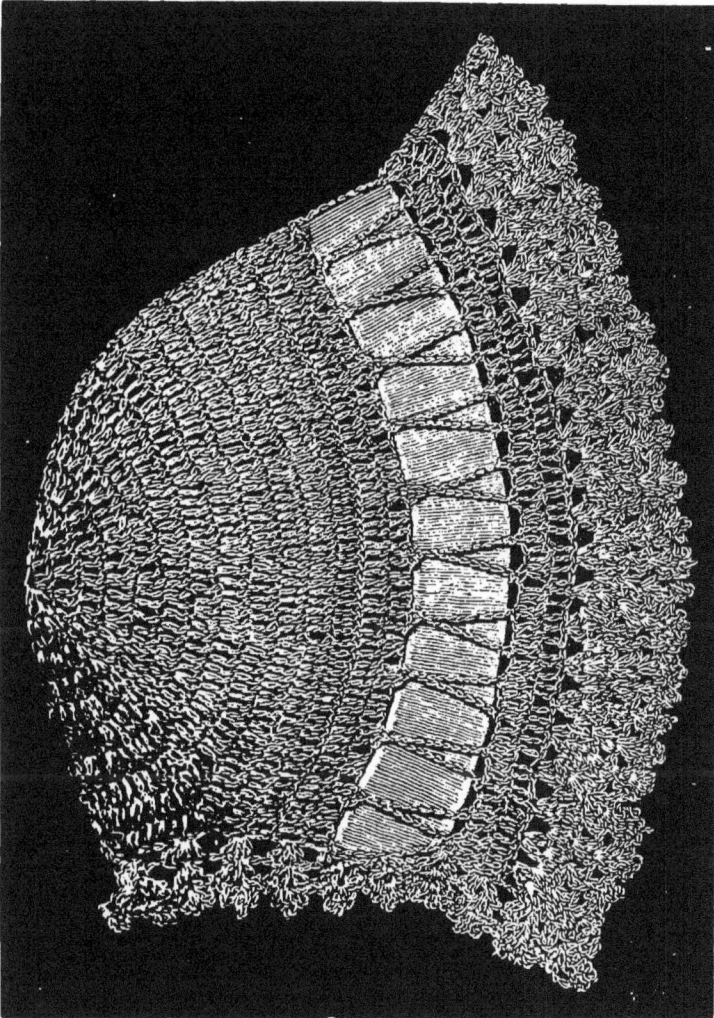

Infant's Bonnet.

16. Turn: ch 9, fasten in top of 1st loop, * ch 3, fasten in top of next loop (in 9th st of 17 ch), repeat from * to the end.

You now have a row of loops for ribbon 1 inch wide, and the bonnet is ready for border.

1. Ch 3, 1 tc in each st of last row.

2. Ch 3, 1 tc in each st of last row.

3. Ch 3, then shell of 4 tc in every 3d tc of last row.

4. Ch 3 ; shell of 4 tc between 2d and 3d tc of sh in last row, sh of 4 tc between shs of last row, repeat across.

5. Ch 3 ; sh of 4 tc in each sh of last row. Work this row of shs all around bonnet. Put the shs at regular intervals across back of neck.

6. Ch 3 ; sh of 4 tc in every sh of last row.

7. Ch 3, fasten with sc in middle of sh of last row, ch 4, fasten in same place, ch 3, fasten in same place, * 1 sc over each of next 3 sts, ch 3, fasten in middle of next sh, ch 4, fasten in same place, ch 3, fasten in same place, repeat all around. This makes a very pretty finishing edge.

Run a ribbon through the loops, weaving it in and out, put a tiny bow at the back, and a larger one on top just back of the border, and you have "a thing of beauty and a joy forever," because it is so serviceable, and when soiled can be easily laundered, which but increases the beauty of linen thread.

One spool will make a bonnet of this size, which is suitable for a child of six months old, hence inexpensiveness is added to its list of virtues.

DEER TIDY.

Use No. 35, 3-cord, 200-yards spools, Barbour's flax thread, either white, écru, or gray, as preferred, with a steel hook, which should be in every case just large enough to carry the thread nicely. It is well to have several sizes of hooks on hand, and those, too, of the best quality.

Make a chain of 260 stitches, turn. The tidy is begun at the bottom, an addition of 5 rows and fringe being made after the work is completed. We begin, therefore, at the 6th row from the bottom, as shown by the illustration.

1. Make 1 tc in the 8th st, * ch 2, pass 2, 1 tc in next st, repeat from * 83 times, thus forming 85 spaces.

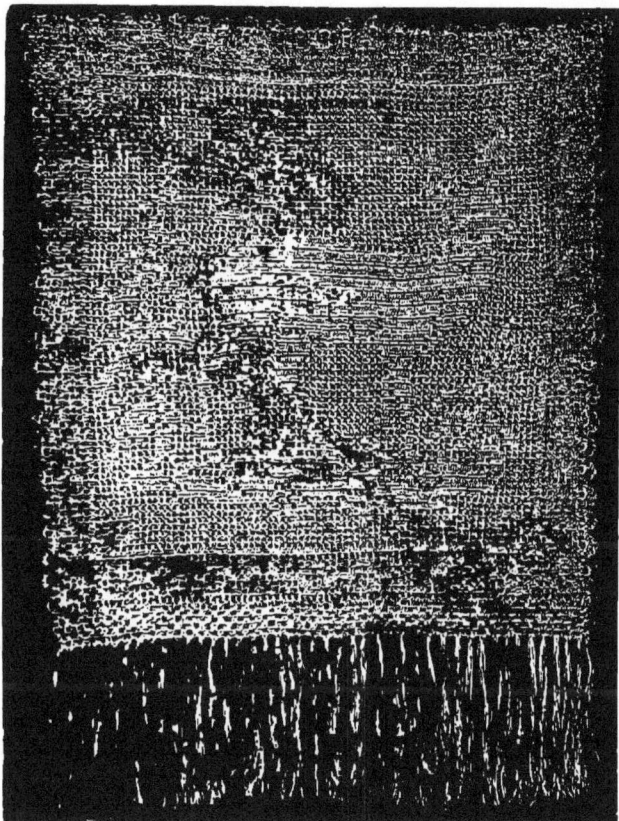

Deer Tidy.

2. Ch 5, tc on next tc, ch. 2, pass 2, tc on next tc (as these spaces are formed always in the same manner the directions may be simplified by referring to them hereafter as " sp ; " also, the solid portion of the pattern is formed of tc, 1 in each st of preceding row),

9 tc (occupying 3 sp), 4 sp, 9 tc, * 2 sp, 3 tc, 2 sp, 9 tc, repeat from * 7 times, 4 sp, 9 tc, 2 sp.

3. Ch 5 to form 1st sp (this is done throughout), 6 tc, 1 sp, 6 tc, 2 sp, * 6 tc, 1 sp, 6 tc, 3 sp, repeat from * 7 times, 6 tc 1 sp, 6 tc, 2 sp, 6 tc, 1 sp, 6 tc, 1 sp, turn.

4. 1 sp, 3 tc, * 3 sp, 12 tc, repeat 9 times, 3 sp, 3 tc, 1 sp.

5. Like 3d row.

6. Like 2d row.

7. 3 sp, 3 tc, 2 sp, 3 tc, 71 sp, 3 tc, 2 sp, 3 tc, 3 sp.

8. 3 sp, 3 tc, 3 sp, 6 tc, 1 sp, 195 tc, 1 sp, 6 tc, 3 sp, 3 tc, 3 sp.

9. 2 sp, 9 tc, 2 sp, 6 tc, 1 sp, 3 tc, 63 sp, 3 tc, 1 sp, 6 tc, 2 sp, 9 tc, 2 sp.

10. 1 sp, 6 tc, 1 sp, 6 tc, 4 sp, 3 tc, 63 sp, 3 tc, 4 sp, 6 tc, 1 sp, 6 tc, 1 sp.

11. 1 sp, 3 tc, 3 sp, 3 tc, 1 sp, 21 tc, 57 sp, 21 tc, 1 sp, 3 tc, 3 sp, 3 tc, 1 sp.

12. 1 sp, 6 tc, 1 sp, 6 tc, 1 sp, 3 tc, 2 sp, 3 tc, 2 sp, 3 tc, 20 sp, 3 tc, 36 sp, 3 tc, 2 sp, 3 tc, 2 sp, 3 tc, 1 sp, 6 tc, 1 sp, 6 tc, 1 sp.

13. 2 sp, 9 tc, 2 sp, 3 tc, 2 sp, 3 tc, 2 sp, 3 tc, 15 sp, 3 tc, 3 sp, 6 tc, 10 sp, 3 tc, 25 sp, 3 tc, 2 sp, 3 tc, 2 sp, 3 tc, 2 sp, 9 tc, 2 sp.

14. 3 sp, 3 tc, 3 sp, 3 tc, 2 sp, 12 tc, * 22 sp, 3 tc, 1 sp, 6 tc, 10 sp, 6 tc, 2 sp, 6 tc, 15 sp, repeat from * back to beginning of row.

15. 1 sp, 3 tc, 1 sp, 3 tc, 1 sp, 3 tc, 1 sp, 3 tc, * 14 sp, 18 tc, 2 sp, 6 tc, 1 sp, 3 tc, 2 sp, 6 tc, 5 sp, 6 tc, 1 sp, 3 tc, 1 sp, 6 tc, 27 sp, repeat back from *.

16. 3 sp, 3 tc, 3 sp, 3 tc, 12 sp, 3 tc, 5 sp, 30 tc, 1 sp, 3 tc, 1 sp, 6 tc, 7 sp, 9 tc, 1 sp, 3 tc, 3 sp, 15 tc, 16 sp, 3 tc, 3 sp, 3 tc, 3 sp.

17. 2 sp, 9 tc, 2 sp, 3 tc, 9 sp, 51 tc, 3 sp, 21 tc, 2 sp, 21 tc, 1 sp, 30 tc, 13 sp, 3 tc, 2 sp, 9 tc, 2 sp.

18. 1 sp, 6 tc, 1 sp, 6 tc, 1 sp, 3 tc, 7 sp, 18 tc, 2 sp, 18 tc, 2 sp, 15 tc, 3 sp, 36 tc, 2 sp, 18 tc, 3 sp, 24 tc, 7 sp, 3 tc, 1 sp, 6 tc, 1 sp, 6 tc, 1 sp.

19. 1 sp, 3 tc, 3 sp, 3 tc, 1 sp, 3 tc, 6 sp, 24 tc, 1 sp, 9 tc, 1 sp, 45 tc, 4 sp, 30 tc, 2 sp, 18 tc, 1 sp, 24 tc, 4 sp, 3 tc, 1 sp, 3 tc, 3 sp, 3 tc, 1 sp.

20. 1 sp, 6 tc, 1 sp, 6 tc, 1 sp, 3 tc, 6 sp, 15 tc, 2 sp, 6 tc, 9 sp, 3 tc, 1 sp, 3 tc, 1 sp, 15 tc, 4 sp, 24 tc, 6 sp, 6 tc, 1 sp, 21 tc, 2 sp, 3 tc, 5 sp, 3 tc, 1 sp, 6 tc, 1 sp, 6 tc, 1 sp.

21. The border ending with 3 tc is now so plainly defined that it will not be necessary to repeat directions each row; after the border, 5 sp, 6 tc, 3 sp, 18 tc, 1 sp, 6 tc, 2 sp, 9 tc, 1 sp, 15 tc, 2 sp, 30 tc, 5 sp, 6 tc, 2 sp, 15 tc, 3 sp, 6 tc, 5 sp, 3 tc, 2 sp; border.

22. Border; 2 sp, 6 tc, 5 sp, 6 tc, 1 sp, 3 tc, 2 sp, 3 tc, 2 sp, 6 tc, 2 sp, 42 tc, 1 sp, 6 tc, 6 sp, 6 tc, 2 sp, 6 tc, 3 sp, 3 tc, 1 sp, 3 tc, 3 sp, 3 tc, 1 sp, 6 tc, 5 sp.

23. Border; 5 sp, 12 tc, 3 sp, 3 tc, 1 sp, 3 tc, 3 sp, 6 tc, 3 sp, 6 tc, 5 sp, 9 tc, 4 sp, 3 tc, 2 sp, 6 tc, 1 sp, 3 tc, 5 sp, 9 tc, 4 sp, 9 tc, 4 sp, 3 tc, 1 sp, 6 tc, 2 sp; border. As the border is made the same on both sides, ending with 3 tc at the beginning of each row, and beginning with 3 tc on the other side, it need not again be mentioned.

24. 3 sp, 3 tc, 1 sp, 3 tc, 4 sp, 6 tc, 5 sp, 6 tc, 6 sp, 3 tc, 1 sp, 3 tc, 1 sp, 3 tc, 4 sp, 3 tc, 1 sp, 6 tc, 6 sp, 3 tc, 4 sp, 3 tc, 6 sp, 6 tc, 2 sp, 9 tc, 2 sp, 3 tc, 3 sp.

25. 3 sp, 6 tc, 3 sp, 6 tc, 1 sp, 3 tc, 4 sp, 3 tc, 2 sp, 3 tc, 4 sp, 3 tc, 7 sp, 9 tc, 4 sp, 3 tc, 1 sp, 3 tc, 2 sp, 3 tc, 6 sp, 6 tc, 4 sp, 6 tc, 2 sp, 3 tc, 1 sp, 9 tc, 3 sp.

26. 4 sp, 3 tc, 1 sp, 9 tc, 1 sp, 6 tc, 2 sp, 3 tc, 1 sp, 6 tc, 8 sp, 6 tc, 1 sp, 6 tc, 3 sp, 6 tc, 8 sp, 3 tc, 4 sp, 3 tc, 2 sp, 6 tc, 1 sp, 3 tc, 1 sp, 3 tc, 1 sp, 3 tc, 2 sp, 3 tc, 1 sp, 6 tc, 3 sp.

27. 4 sp, 12 tc, 2 sp, 3 tc, 1 sp, 12 tc, 3 sp, 3 tc, 3 sp, 6 tc, 9 sp, 6 tc, 2 sp, 3 tc, 3 sp, 3 tc, 8 sp, 6 tc, 1 sp, 3 tc, 1 sp, 3 tc, 1 sp, 3 tc, 1 sp, 15 tc, 4 sp.

28. 5 sp, 9 tc, 1 sp, 3 tc, 1 sp, 12 tc, 2 sp, 3 tc, 7 sp, 3 tc, 6 sp, 6 tc, 10 sp, 6 tc, 3 sp, 3 tc, 4 sp, 9 tc, 1 sp, 6 tc, 1 sp, 6 tc, 6 sp.

29. 7 sp, 3 tc, 1 sp, 15 tc, 5 sp, 6 tc, 2 sp, 3 tc, 12 sp, 3 tc, 6 sp, 6 tc, 6 sp, 3 tc, 3 sp, 9 tc, 1 sp, 12 tc, 2 sp, 3 tc, 3 sp.

30. 3 sp, 6 tc, 2 sp, 9 tc, 1 sp, 6 tc, 4 sp, 3 tc, 6 sp, 3 tc, 6 sp, 6 tc, 12 sp, 6 tc, 1 sp, 6 tc, 3 sp, 3 tc, 5 sp, 6 tc, 2 sp, 3 tc, 5 sp.

31. 3 sp, 9 tc, 2 sp, 3 tc, 2 sp, 3 tc, 1 sp, 3 tc, 1 sp, 3 tc, 3 sp, 6 tc, 1 sp, 6 tc, 13 sp, 3 tc, 6 sp, 9 tc, 4 sp, 3 tc, 5 sp, 6 tc, 1 sp, 3 tc, 2 sp, 6 tc, 2 sp, 3 tc, 1 sp.

32. 1 sp, 6 tc, 3 sp, 3 tc, 1 sp, 3 tc, 1 sp, 3 tc, 3 sp, 3 tc, 2 sp, 3 tc, 3 sp, 3 tc, 2 sp, 3 tc, 5 sp, 6 tc, 13 sp, 3 tc, 1 sp, 9 tc, 4 sp, 12 tc, 1 sp, 3 tc, 2 sp, 6 tc, 5 sp.

33. 7 sp, 3 tc, 1 sp, 12 tc, 6 sp, 9 tc, 1 sp, 3 tc, 13 sp, 6 tc, 4 sp, 6 tc, 5 sp, 6 tc, 2 sp, 6 tc, 2 sp, 6 tc, 1 sp, 3 tc, 3 sp, 9 tc, 1 sp.

34. 1 sp, 9 tc, 4 sp, 6 tc, 1 sp, 3 tc, 1 sp, 6 tc, 2 sp, 6 tc, 4 sp, 6 tc, 4 sp, 9 tc, 13 sp, 3 tc, 1 sp, 6 tc, 10 sp, 6 tc, 8 sp.

35. 3 sp, 6 tc, 3 sp, 3 tc, 11 sp, 9 tc, 14 sp, 12 tc, 3 sp, 3 tc, 4 sp, 9 tc, 3 sp, 9 tc, 1 sp, 3 tc, 3 sp, 3 tc, 1 sp, 6 tc, 2 sp.

36. 3 sp, 12 tc, 3 sp, 6 tc, 6 sp, 9 tc, 3 sp, 3 tc, 4 sp, 9 tc, 14 sp, 9 tc, 8 sp, 6 tc, 2 sp, 3 tc, 1 sp, 6 tc, 4 sp.

37. 6 sp, 6 tc, 1 sp, 6 tc, 7 sp, 3 tc, 1 sp, 12 tc, 12 sp, 9 tc, 8 sp, 12 tc, 7 sp, 3 tc, 1 sp, 3 tc, 1 sp, 9 tc, 4 sp.

38. 1 sp, 3 tc, 3 sp, 15 tc, 6 sp, 3 tc, 1 sp, 21 tc, 5 sp, 12 tc, 11 sp, 12 tc, 1 sp, 3 tc, 9 sp, 6 tc, 7 sp.

39. 4 sp, 3 tc, 2 sp, 3 tc, 9 sp, 3 tc, 1 sp, 18 tc, 9 sp, 15 tc, 4 sp, 18 tc, 3 sp, 6 tc, 1 sp, 3 tc, 3 sp, 12 tc, 1 sp, 3 tc, 1 sp, 6 tc, 1 sp.

40. 2 sp, 12 tc, 2 sp, 6 tc, 1 sp, 3 tc, 1 sp, 12 tc, 4 sp, 18 tc, 3 sp, 12 tc, 2 sp, 12 tc, 1 sp, 6 tc, 1 sp, 18 tc, 1 sp, 6 tc, 9 sp, 6 tc, 5 sp.

41. 6 sp, 3 tc, 9 sp, 3 tc, 1 sp, 21 tc, 1 sp, 27 tc, 6 sp, 21 tc, 5 sp, 18 tc, 1 sp, 15 tc, 4 sp.

42. 7 sp, 6 tc, 1 sp, 12 tc, 8 sp, 21 tc, 1 sp, 30 tc, 1 sp, 9 tc, 1 sp, 18 tc, 1 sp, 6 tc, 8 sp, 3 tc, 6 sp.

43. 5 sp, 3 tc, 7 sp, 12 tc, 1 sp, 18 tc, 1 sp, 9 tc, 1 sp, 6 tc, 1 sp, 21 tc, 1 sp, 21 tc, 11 sp, 3 tc, 1 sp, 3 tc, 3 sp, 3 tc, 4 sp.

44. 4 sp, 6 tc, 3 sp, 3 tc, 12 sp, 24 tc, 1 sp, 9 tc, 1 sp, 6 tc, 1 sp, 6 tc, 1 sp, 9 tc, 1 sp, 21 tc, 1 sp, 9 tc, 13 sp.

45. 13 sp, 9 tc, 1 sp, 33 tc, 1 sp, 6 tc, 1 sp, 6 tc, 1 sp, 9 tc, 1 sp, 24 tc, 3 sp, 3 tc, 2 sp, 3 tc, 5 sp, 3 tc, 1 sp, 3 tc, 1 sp, 6 tc, 4 sp.

46. 1 sp, 6 tc, 1 sp, 12 tc, 4 sp, 3 tc, 1 sp, 6 tc, 1 sp, 6 tc, 3 sp, 24 tc, 1 sp, 9 tc, 1 sp, 6 tc, 1 sp, 9 tc, 1 sp, 30 tc, 1 sp, 15 tc, 11 sp.

47. 10 sp, 18 tc, 1 sp, 39 tc, 1 sp, 9 tc, 1 sp, 9 tc, 1 sp, 27 tc, 3 sp, 18 tc, 2 sp, 3 tc, 1 sp, 9 tc, 1 sp, 6 tc, 2 sp.

48. 6 sp, 12 tc, 1 sp, 12 tc, 4 sp, 3 tc, 1 sp, 27 tc, 1 sp, 12 tc, 1 sp, 69 tc, 10 sp.

49. 9 sp, 84 tc, 1 sp, 30 tc, 1 sp, 3 tc, 6 sp, 3 tc, 1 sp, 9 tc, 8 sp.

50. 3 sp, 6 tc, 1 sp, 3 tc, 2 sp, 9 tc, 7 sp, 6 tc, 1 sp, 99 tc, 2 sp, 9 tc, 9 sp.

51. 9 sp, 15 tc, 1 sp, 93 tc, 1 sp, 6 tc, 11 sp, 3 tc, 1 sp, 9 tc, 4 sp.

52. 6 sp, 9 tc, 1 sp, 3 tc, 10 sp, 90 tc, 1 sp, 24 tc, 9 sp.

53. 9 sp, 12 tc, 1 sp, 6 tc, 3 sp, 9 tc, 1 sp, 72 tc, 5 sp, 3 tc, 1 sp, 3 tc, 1 sp, 3 tc, 1 sp, 3 tc, 1 sp, 3 tc, 8 sp.

54. 9 sp, 6 tc, 1 sp, 12 tc, 8 sp, 48 tc, 13 sp, 3 tc, 1 sp, 15 tc, 9 sp.

55. 5 sp, 6 tc, 2 sp, 3 tc, 2 sp, 9 tc, 17 sp, 33 tc, 12 sp, 12 tc, 10 sp.

56. 10 sp, 6 tc, 13 sp, 3 tc, 28 sp, 6 tc, 1 sp, 15 tc, 1 sp, 6 tc, 4 sp.

57. 5 sp, 24 tc, 1 sp, 3 tc, 28 sp, 3 tc, 2 sp, 3 tc, 1 sp, 3 tc, 9 sp, 3 tc, 10 sp.

58. 11 sp, 3 tc, 8 sp, 15 tc, 1 sp, 3 tc, 3 sp, 6 tc, 22 sp, 3 tc, 1 sp, 21 tc, 6 sp.

59. 7 sp, 9 tc, 1 sp, 12 tc, 23 sp, 6 tc, 2 sp, 3 tc, 2 sp, 6 tc, 2 sp, 3 tc, 7 sp, 3 tc, 1 sp, 6 tc, 8 sp.

60. 10 sp, 6 tc, 1 sp, 6 tc, 5 sp, 9 tc, 3 sp, 9 tc, 26 sp, 21 tc; 7 sp.

61. 8 sp, 24 tc, 23 sp, 3 tc, 2 sp, 6 tc, 11 sp, 9 tc, 11 sp.

62. 11 sp, 3 tc, 14 sp, 3 tc, 4 sp, 3 tc, 20 sp, 3 tc, 1 sp, 3 tc, 1 sp, 15 tc, 8 sp.

63. 7 sp, 6 tc, 1 sp, 3 tc, 1 sp, 6 tc, 1 sp, 9 tc, 16 sp, 3 tc, 2 sp, 12 tc, 1 sp, 3 tc, 1 sp, 3 tc, 11 sp, 3 tc, 12 sp.

64. 12 sp, 6 tc, 8 sp, 3 tc, 1 sp, 6 tc, 1 sp, 3 tc, 1 sp, 6 tc, 1 sp, 9 tc, 19 sp, 6 tc, 2 sp, 6 tc, 1 sp, 6 tc, 6 sp.

65. 9 sp, 9 tc, 2 sp, 9 tc, 18 sp, 9 tc, 2 sp, 12 tc, 1 sp, 6 tc, 9 sp, 6 tc, 11 sp.

66. 12 sp, 3 tc, 7 sp, 3 tc, 2 sp, 9 tc, 1 sp, 3 tc, 1 sp, 3 tc, 18 sp, 15 tc, 1 sp, 3 tc, 4 sp, 6 tc, 8 sp.

67. 6 sp, 9 tc, 5 sp, 3 tc, 1 sp, 9 tc, 1 sp, 9 tc, 14 sp, 9 tc, 1 sp, 3 tc, 4 sp, 9 tc, 7 sp, 3 tc, 12 sp.

68. 13 sp, 3 tc, 7 sp, 9 tc, 1 sp, 3 tc, 1 sp, 3 tc, 3 sp, 6 tc, 12 sp, 9 tc, 1 sp, 3 tc, 2 sp, 3 tc, 6 sp, 9 tc, 7 sp.

69. 6 sp, 6 tc, 1 sp, 3 tc, 11 sp, 3 tc, 2 sp, 3 tc, 14 sp, 6 tc, 1 sp, 6 tc, 25 sp.

70. 23 sp, 6 tc, 1 sp, 9 tc, 33 sp, 3 tc, 6 sp.

71. 5 sp, 9 tc, 34 sp, 9 tc, 24 sp.

72. 2 sp, 12 tc, 55 sp, 3 tc, 1 sp, 3 tc, 5 sp.

73. 7 sp, 3 tc, 55 sp, 3 tc, 2 sp, 3 tc, 2 sp.

74. 2 sp, 3 tc, 2 sp, 3 tc, 54 sp, 3 tc, 8 sp.

75. 9 tc (after the 3 tc of border), 60 sp, 18 tc (before 3 tc of border).

76. Like 10th row.

77. Like 9th row.

78. Like 8th row.

79. Like 7th row.

Repeat thus back to the 1st row, which — the 85th row of tidy — will be composed entirely of spaces. This completes the pattern.

Five rows are now added to the bottom or lower edge of tidy.

1. Fasten the thread in 1st sp, in 3d st of 5 ch, ch 5, 1 tc in next tc, 1 under ch and 1 in next tc, ch 2, miss 2, 1 tc in next; continue across, alternating 1 sp, 3 tc.

2. Ch 3, 2 tc under 1st ch loop, * ch 2, miss 3 tc, 3 tc under next ch loop, repeat from * across, and repeat the 2d row 3 times.

Finish the top and sides with a scallop made as follows: After making 5th row, turn, and in the space at end of 3d row (of the 5 added rows at bottom) * make 2 tc, ch 3, 2 dtc, ch 3, 2 dtc, ch 3, 2 tc, * fasten with 1 dc in sp at end of 1st of the 5 rows, repeat from * to * under next sp on edge, fasten under next, and so continue around to the opposite lower corner. Cut threads of the linen 11 or 12 inches long, and 7 or 8 in each cluster, double each cluster in the middle, put the doubled end through under 2 ch at the bottom, draw the ends through, and pull up. Make a loop of fringe in this way in every space across the bottom.

In No. 1 of the Prize Series the illustration of this "Deer Tidy" was intended to illustrate "Cross-stitch in Crochet," but by some misunderstanding a cross-stitch pattern for working on gingham was inserted under this head. By observing the formation of the spaces and solid squares (3 tc) in directions for the tidy, any cross-stitch design may be copied with the crochet needle. Entire curtains, bedspreads, pillow-shams, etc., are made in this way.

END FOR SCARF.

[Contributed by Mrs. H. J. FLEURY, Newport News, Va.]

Use No. 25, 3-cord, 200-yards spools, Barbour's écru flax thread, and a rather coarse hook.

1. * Ch 15, fasten with sc back into 6th st, ch 3, 12 tc in loop; repeat from * 3 times, ch 15, fasten back into 6th st, ch 3, 24 tc in

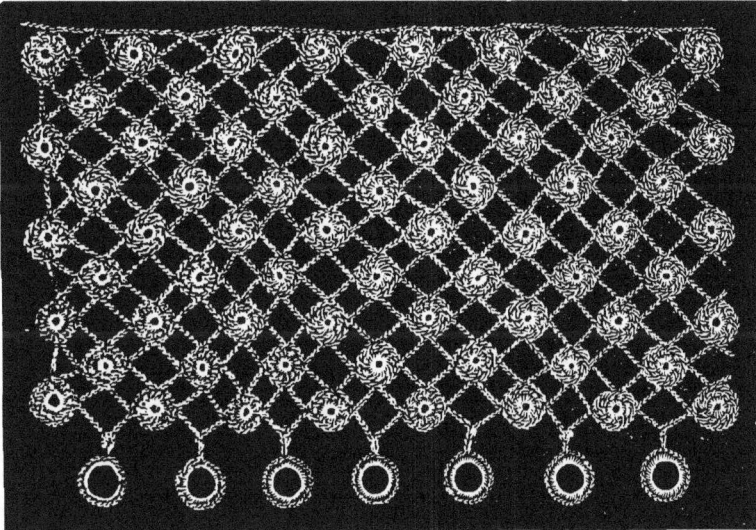

End for Scarf.

loop, fasten with sc in top of 3 ch and around the connecting ch, forming a complete wheel.

2. * Ch 11, fasten with sc in top of last tc in next wheel, make

1 2 tc in loop, forming another wheel ; repeat from * until you have filled the next 3 wheels, ch 13.

3. Fasten into 6th st of wheel, ch 15, fasten back into 6th st of ch, ch 3, 6 tc in loop, fasten to centre of 11 ch in last row, 6 tc in loop, ch 5, fasten with sc to centre st of next wheel, * ch 15, fasten in 6th st, ch 3, 5 tc in loop, fasten to centre of 11 ch, 6 tc in loop, ch 5, fasten in centre of next wheel, repeat twice from *, ch 15, fasten back into 7th st to form a picot.

4. Ch 11, * fasten into top of tc in half-wheel, 12 tc in loop, ch 11, repeat from * to last wheel, then fasten the 11 ch into 13 ch in last row, and begin next row with 15 ch.

Repeat until the work is long enough for your scarf or for purpose designed, then cover brass rings with the thread in double crochet and fasten into the picots at the bottom. This would be very pretty worked of the embroidery flax thread, size oo.

TIDIES IN HAIRPIN-WORK.

[Contributed by Miss BERTHA WEABER, Vineland, N.J.]

I wish particularly to speak of the excellence of Barbour's flax threads when used in hairpin lace. I have just completed some very pretty tidies, dainty and flimsy as cobwebs, but strong, almost, as wire.

Nearly every one is doubtless more or less familiar with the method of making hairpin or maltese work, but a description may be of advantage to a few. A hairpin is required of the width you wish to make the loops, but with very stiff prongs which will not bend, and also a crochet-hook. Make a loop of the thread around the pin, holding thread at back, pin in left hand, and crochet-hook in right ; have the loop near the end of prongs, as the pin is held, prongs upward. Put the hook between the prongs, upward, under the nearest thread, take up thread, draw through, then draw through st on hook ; this forms half the knot. * Turn the pin over, from right to left,

letting the thread pass around the prong, and bringing the hook over
the point of prong to front again, put hook under the upper cross
thread at left of centre, draw thread through, then draw through the
2 sts on hook. Repeat from * to the length desired. This is for
single work. For double work, as for tidies, etc., put hook under
both threads at left of centre instead of upper thread, and for particularly heavy work, such as heading for fringe, the. working thread
is sometimes used double. As the work proceeds, slip the loops
down toward the round part of pin; when the latter is full, slip off
the work and replace a few loops in order to continue.

Tidy No. 1. Use Barbour's flax thread, écru or white, as preferred,
No. 70, 3-cord, 200-yards spools, embroidery flax thread, size 00,
shade 55, and ribbon to match, No. 3 or No. 4. A pin or staple 1½
inches wide at points of prongs will be needed, and fine steel hook.

Make a strip of hairpin-work (putting hook under both threads)
54 loops long; insert crochet-hook in all the loops along one side,
draw a thread through and fasten firmly together. This forms a
rosette with solid centre and loose loops on the edge. Next, with
the embroidery thread, which should be either loosely wound or
carefully drawn from the skein, catch 3 loops together, fastening with
1 dc. Make a double knot-st, as elsewhere described, catch with 1
dc in next 3 loops, drawn together, and repeat all around. There
should be 18 double knot-sts in all. Next work around with single
knot-sts, fastening each in the centre knot of preceding row. The
loops should be about ½ inch long. Take 9 of these rosettes (or
more if a larger tidy is wanted) and join them by crocheting together where the edges touch. Finish off with a pretty bow of ribbon on each upper corner, and finish lower edge with a knotted
fringe. When completed you have a tidy that for strength and deli-
cacy of appearance cannot easily be outrivalled.

Tidy No. 2. Another beauty is made as follows: Make 3 strips of
hairpin-work 76 loops long; take up four loops on hook and draw
them through 4 loops on 2d strip, then draw these last through 4
more on 1st strip, and so continue, back and forth, to the end, using
loops on one side of each strip only. When at the bottom fasten

the last 4 down by drawing a loose piece of thread through them
and the strip of lace, to keep from pulling out. Take the 3d strip
and join to the 2d strip as 1st and 2d were joined. This makes a
complete lace strip. Four of these are used for a tidy. Take 3
pieces of No. 16 satin ribbon, each ⅜ yard in length, and stitch the
lace on them, leaving an equal space at top and bottom of ribbon;
sew the lace fast through the rib in the latter, letting the loops extend

Tidy No. 3.

over the ribbon. When this is done, finish off the top by folding the
ribbon over on the wrong side and joining the edges to form a point
on each piece of ribbon. Sew a medium-sized plush ball on each
end and on each strip of lace, 7 in all. For the bottom use larger
ornaments, 4 in number, sew on each strip of lace, ravel the
ribbon even with body of tidy, and tie the ravelled ends to
tassels.

For this tidy I used Barbour's flax thread, No. 60, 3-cord, 200-yards spools, and turquoise blue ribbon and ornaments.

Tidy No. 3. This is of heavier material. Barbour's flax thread, écru, No. 35, 3-cord, 200-yards spools, 1 yard yellow satin ribbon 2 inches wide, and 1⅔ yards satin ribbon, same shade, 1 inch wide. A staple 2 inches wide will be needed. Two spools of thread will be sufficient. Make a strip 450 loops long; on one side (not the side you finish from the hairpin, but the other side) put the hook through 5 loops, fasten with 1 dc, ch 6, pick up 5 loops and fasten as before, and repeat until you have 43 clusters. Then leave 20 loops and work as before until you have 43 clusters on this side, which will leave 20 loops for the other end. Join the strip by doubling in half; work in the centre by taking up 5 loops (10 threads), drawing 5 loops from opposite side through the 5 on your needle, and so continue, drawing 5 loops from alternate sides through the 5 on needle until you reach the end; then draw 10 through 10 and fasten, leaving the outside ends of 20 loops for bottom and top. Make 3 strips in this way, join by sewing the crocheted edges to the narrow ribbon strips (each 30 inches long), turn under and hem the raw ends of the latter, then tie a pretty bow of the wide ribbon around the centre of tidy, drawing it together.

Very quickly made, and very pretty; the flax threads are lovely for them, rich and silky.

With a little ingenuity very nandsome throws, toilet-cushion covers, night-robe sachets, etc., can be made with this lace.

CHEMISE YOKE.

[Contributed by Mrs. ANNA P. CLARK, Colmar, Pa.]

Materials: 2 spools Barbour's flax thread, No. 70, 3-cord, 200-yards spools, and a fine steel hook.

The yoke is formed by 36 wheels,— 7 for front, 7 for back, 6 over each shoulder, 4 under the arm, and 1 under joining of 4th and 5th (under the arm) to form point of sleeve.

Wheels are begun in centre by 9 ch joined in a ring.

hemi-e Yoke.

1. Ch 3, 17 tc in ring, fasten with sc in top of 3 ch.

2. Ch 4, * 1 tc in next tc, ch 1, repeat from * 16 times, fasten in 3d of 4 ch.

3. Ch 3, 2 tc under 1 ch, * ch 1, 3 tc under next 1 ch, repeat from * 16 times, ch 1 and fasten in top of 3 ch.

4. * Ch 9, 1 sc in 1 ch between groups of 3 tc, repeat from * 17 times, break thread and fasten. In the last row of each wheel after the 1st, * ch 4, catch with sc in centre of 9 ch of preceding wheel, ch 4, fasten under 1 ch in wheel you are working, repeat from last * 3 times, then finish the wheel. Join the wheels together as worked, in this way, to shape the yoke.

For edge around top and sleeves :

1. 1 sc in last loop of 9 ch next to where last wheel of front is joined to first of shoulder, ch 9, 3 dtc in next loop (where joined to shoulder), keeping last st of each on needle, 3 dtc in next loop, keeping last st of each on needle, then draw thread through all at once, draw thread through st on hook, to fasten, ch 9, fasten with 1 sc in centre of next loop, and continue all around the yoke, making the groups of dtc as described between the wheels.

2. 3 tc in each loop of 9 ch; repeat all around.

3. 2 tc separated by 3 ch in centre tc of 3 tc; repeat all around.

4. 3 tc in each 3 ch; repeat all around.

5. Ch 7, fasten with 1 sc in centre tc of 3 tc; repeat all around.

6. 6 tc in 1st loop of 7 ch, * fasten with 1 sc in next loop, 6 tc in next loop; repeat all around.

For lower part of yoke :

1. Same as 1st row of top.

2. Same as 2d row of top, with exception of the point of sleeve. Make 3 tc in 1st 3 loops after groups of dtc, and 6 tc in each of next 8 loops; then 3 tc in next 3 loops, and continue.

3 and 4. Same as 3d and 4th rows of top.

5. Ch 3, fasten in centre of 3 tc; repeat.

6. 3 tc in each 3 ch; repeat.

The edge of sleeves is finished same as the neck, and narrow ribbon run in the spaces formed by ch of 7.

Very easy, but pretty.

HARLEQUIN TIDY.

[Contributed by Miss ALICE M. ROBINSON, Gloucester, Mass.]

This tidy may be made' of one color flax thread, No. 25, 3-cord, 200-yards spools, or in 3 colors (for a " harlequin " tidy), blue, yellow, and red.

Begin with the large wheels, which are of blue, choosing a steel hook large enough to carry the thread easily, but not so large as to make loose work.

Ch 14, join with 1 sc in 1st st of ch.

1. Ch 2 to take place of a stc, 23 stc in ring, join with 1 sc to top of 2 ch.

2. Ch 2 for 1st stc, 1 stc in each of next 2 sts, * ch 10, 1 stc in each of next 3 sts; repeat from * until 18 ch loops are formed, fastening the last loop of 10 ch with 1 sc in top of 2 ch.

3. 1 dc in middle of 3 stc, * then under loop of 10 ch following work 5 stc, 2 tc, 2 dtc, ch 4, 2 dtc, 2 tc, 5 stc, 1 dc in 2d of 3 stc of last round ; repeat from * 7 times, fastening in 2d stc.

4. Work up to loop of 4 ch with 1 sc in each st (or break thread and fasten in as preferred), 1 dc under 4 ch, * ch 10, 1 dc under same 4 ch, repeat from * 4 times, ch 5, remove hook, put it through centre of 10 ch just made, draw the dropped st through, ch 5, 1 dc under next 4 ch, ch 5, drop st, put hook through top of 5 ch last made, draw dropped st through, ch 5, 1 dc under 4 ch, ch 10, 1 dc under same ch, and so continue around the rosette, finishing with 1 extra dtc (thread over 3 times), under 1st loop of 4 ch, joined to centre of 1st loop of 10 ch.

5. The last fastening being between the 2 groups of 3, * ch 3, 1 dc in top of next loop of 10 ch, repeat from * twice, ch 3, 1 dc where groups of 3 are joined, then repeat from * all around, thus separating each loop with 3 ch, fastened by 1 dc. Fasten last 3 ch between the groups of 3.

6. Ch 3 for 1 tc, * ch 4, 1 dc over dc in top of 10 ch, ch 4, 1 dc under 3 ch, ch 4, 1 dc in next dc, ch 3, dc under 3 ch, ch 3, dc in dc, ch 3, 1 tc in next dc (between groups of 3) ; repeat from * all around, fastening in top of 3 ch with 1 sc.

Harlequin Tidy.

This completes the large rosette or wheel, of which 9 are required. These may be joined as worked, if desired, or with needle and thread. To join when working, in making the last row of 2d and subsequent rosettes, make 2 of the 3 ch on one side of centre dc, put hook through corresponding ch of previous rosette, draw thread through, ch 2, dc in dc, ch 2, fasten as before to corresponding ch of preceding rosette, ch 1, and proceed.

The small rosettes or squares, joining the large ones, are of yellow. Ch 10, join.

1. Ch 2, 14 stc in ring, join to top of 2 ch.

2. 1 dc in 1st st, * ch 10, 1 dc in next, repeat twice from *, 1 dc in next st, repeat from * all around, fastening last 10 ch with 1 dc close to 1st dc.

3. Work up to top of 10 ch with 1 sc in each st (or, better, in making the last ch loop, ch 5, then make 1 extra dtc in next st, which will bring you to the top of loop), * ch 3, 1 dc in top of next loop ; repeat all around, fastening last 3 ch in top of loop where you started.

4. It will be noted that this rosette consists of 12 loops, divided into groups of 3 by 2 dc between. Make 1 dc in the dc at top of centre loop, ch 3, join to centre dc in scallop of large rosette, work back on 3 ch with 1 sc in each of 2d and 3d sts, 1 dc under 3 ch, ch 3, 1 dc on dc, ch 3, 1 dc under 3 ch, and so continue, fastening the ch of 3 with 2 dc over the 2 dc in the ring below, where the ch loops are fastened, and joining to each of the larger rosettes by the centre of 3 loops. Make half-wheels for the sides, 2 for each, consisting of 6 ch loops, making and joining them as described, and quarter-wheels (3 loops each), for the corners, joining to corner rosette over middle loop.

For the border, which is of red :

1. Fasten in under the ring of quarter-wheel in corner, 7 dc in ring, ch 7, 1 dc at end of ch loop of quarter-wheel, ch 16, 1 dc under 2d loop of 4 ch in large rosette, ch 2, 1 dc under next ch loop, ch 16, 1 dc at top of ch loop in half-wheel, ch 72, dc under ring, ch 7, 1 dc in top of ch loop, and continue thus all around the tidy, making a straight chain. Some allowance must be made for working tightly or loosely : the chain should be equal in length to the space between fastenings.

2. Stc all around, working 3 or 4 extra at the corners to make them square. Begin with 2 ch, and join last stc to top of this.

3. 3 tc in centre of 5 stc at corner, * ch 3, miss 3, 3 tc in next 3 sts, repeat all around, putting 3 tc in 1 st at corners. Join last 3 ch to top of 1st tc.

4. 1 sc in each of next 3 st, ch 3 (for 1 tc), 2 tc under 3 ch, ch 3, 3 tc under next 3 ch, repeat all around, making a ch of 6 at corners. Join last 6 ch to top of 3 ch, at beginning.

5. Like 2d row. Ch 2, 1 stc in every st of previous row, with 3 in 1 st at corners; join to top of 2 ch.

6. 1 dc in st over 1st of 3 tc below, * ch 14, turn, miss 1, 1 dc in each of 13 sts, miss 1 of foundation, 1 sc in each of next 5, ch 3, miss 2, 2 dtc separated by 3 ch in next st, ch 3, miss 2, 1 sc in each of 5 sts, and repeat from *. At the corners, miss but 1 st in half-circle, and but 3 between it and next figure.

7. After fastening last 3 ch, 1 sc in each of 3 sts, then * 1 stc in each of 13 sts, 3 dc in top st, then 13 stc down other side of 13 dc, taking back loop of st, miss 2 of 5 sts of foundation, fasten in next, 7 stc under 1st 3 ch, 8 stc under next 3 ch, 7 stc under next 3 ch, miss 2 sc, dc in next, and repeat from *.

8. Fasten in yellow in centre of 8 dc filling middle sp of half-wheel, ch 4, miss 2, 1 extra dtc in next, ch 6, 1 dc in 2d st (thus forming a 5 ch picot), * ch 1, 1 extra dtc in last of 13 stc, * ch 1, 1 p, ch 1, 1 extra dtc in following dc, repeat from 2d * twice, ch 1, 1 p, ch 1, extra dtc in 1st stc following, ch 1, 1 p, ch 1, 1 extra dtc in 2d of 8 stc (in centre sp), ch 4, miss 2, 2 dc in next 2 sts, ch 4, join to top of last extra dtc by slip-stitch, miss 2, 1 extra dtc in next st, ch 1, 1 p, ch 1, repeat from 1st * all around, finishing the top of half-circle with 1 extra dtc and 4 ch.

Make 4 tassels of all the colors, cutting the threads 4 inches long, doubling and tying securely. Fasten 1 to each corner.

This tidy is showy and durable. It makes a very nice piano-stool cover.

LADY'S NECKTIE.

FIRST PRIZE ARTICLE.

[Contributed by Miss M. S. BROWN, Woburn, Mass.]

Materials: Barbour's flax thread, white, No. 100, 3-cord, 200-yards spools, and 2 needles, No. 16.

Cast on 73 stitches.

1. K 4, * k 2, o, n, k 1, o, n, k 3, n, o, k 1, n, o, k 1, * k 2, n, o, * k 1, o, n, k 3, n, o, repeat from last * until 25 sts remain on left-hand needle, k 1, knit back from 3d * to edge.

2. K 2, o, k 2, * k 3, o, n, k 1, o, n, k 1, n, o, k 1, n, o, k 2, * k 1, n, o, k 1, * k 2, o, n, k 1, n, o, k 1, repeat from last * until but 25 stitches remain on needle, k 1, knit back from 3d *.

3. K 2, o, k 1, n, o, * k 1, o, n, k 1, o, n, k 1, o, sl, n and b o, k 1, n, o, k 1, n, o, * n, o, k 2, * k 3, o, sl, n and b, o, k 2, repeat from last *, k 1, knit back from 3d *.

4. K 2, o, k 1, n, o, k 1, * k 2, o, n, k 1, o, sl, n and b, o, k 1, o, sl, n and b, o, k 1, n, o, k 1, * k 4, * k 2, n, o, k 1, o, n, k 1, repeat from last *, k 1, knit back from 3d *.

5. K 2, o, k 1, n, o, k 2, * k 3, o, n, k 1, o, n, k 1, n, o, k 1, n, o, k 2, * k 2, o, n, * k 1, n, o, k 3, o, n, repeat from last *, k 1, knit back from 3d *.

6. K 2, o, k 1, n, o, k 3, * o, n, k 2, o, n, k 1, o, sl, n and b, o, k 1, n, o, k 3, * o, n, k 1, o, * sl, n and b, o, k 5, o, repeat from last *, sl, n and b, knit back from 3d *.

7. K 3, o, n, k 1, o, n, k 1, * k 2, n, o, k 1, n, o, k 3, o, n, k 1, o, n, k 1, * k 2, n, o, * k 1, o, n, k 3, n, o, repeat from last *, k 1, knit back from 3d *.

8. K 1, n, k 1, o, n, k 1, o, n, * k 1, n, o, k 1, n, o, k 5, o, n, k 1, o, n, * k 1, n, o, k 1, * k 2, o, n, k 1, n, o, k 1, repeat from last *, k 1, knit back from 3d *.

9. K 1, n, k 1, o, n, k 1, o, * sl, n and b, o, k 1, n, o, k 1, n, o, k 1, o, n, k 1, o, n, k 1, o, * sl, n and b, o, k 2, * k 3, o, sl, n and b, o, k 2, repeat from last *, k 1, knit back from 3d *.

10. K 1, n, k 1, o, k 3 tog, o, * k 1, o, k 3 tog, o, k 1, n, o, k 3,

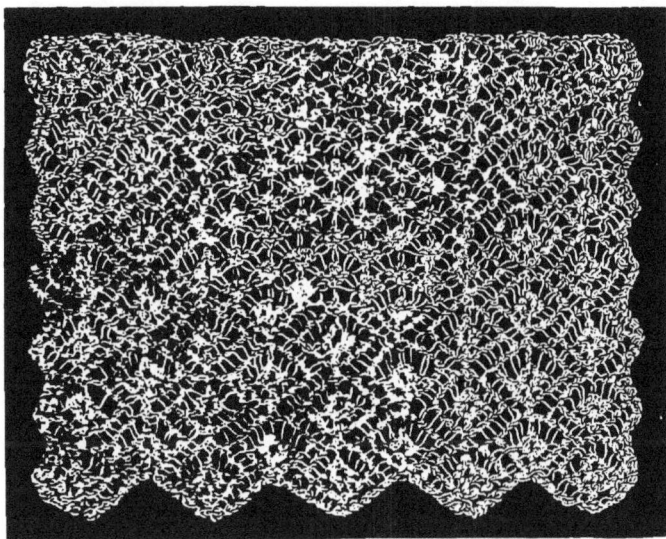

Lady's Necktie.

o, n, k 1, o, k 3 tog, o, * k 4, * k 2, n, o, k 1, o, n, k 1, repeat from last *, k 1, knit back from 3d *.

11. K 1, n, k 1, o, n, * k 1, n, o, k 1, n, o, k 5, o, n, k 1, o, n, * k 2, o, n, * k 1, n, o, k 3, o, n, repeat from last *, k 1, knit back from 3d *.

12. K 1, n, k 1, o, * sl, n and b, o, k 1, n, o, k 3, o, n, k 2, o, n, k 1, o, * sl, n and b, o, k 5, o, repeat from last *, sl, n and b, o, knit back from 3d *.

Repeat these 12 rows 33 times, then begin at 1st row, knit to 2d *, repeat from 1st to 2d * until 5 stitches remain, k 1, knit back from 1st * to edge. Knit the remaining rows in same manner, knitting 1 after repeating in 1st to 7th rows inclusive, also in the 10th and 11th. In the 9th and 12th, sl, n and b, then knit back from 1st *. Knit 2 scallops and 5 rows on the 3d in the same manner; 6th row the same, except k 3 instead of sl, n and b.

7. K 3, o, n, k 1, o, n, * k 3, knit back from *; do not slip last st off left-hand needle.

8. K 1, n, k 1, o, n, k 1, o, n, * k 1, knit back from *.

9. K 1, n, k 1, o, n, k 1, o, * sl, n and b, knit back from *.

10. K 1, n, k 1, o, sl, n and b, o, * k 1, knit back from *.

11. K 1, n, k 1, o, n, * k 1, knit back from *.

12. K 1, n, k 1, o, *, slip, n and b, knit back from *.

13. K 1, n, k 3, n, k 1.

14. N, sl, n and b, n.

15. Sl, n and b, fasten off.

Finish remaining points in same manner, beginning with 7th row.

Take up the same number of sts on other end as first cast on, and knit the other half of necktie in same way as already described. It may be made wider or narrower by adding or decreasing 16 stitches, which is the number required for a pattern. A handkerchief knitted in this way would be very delicate and pretty.

INFANT'S KNITTED HOOD.

SECOND PRIZE ARTICLE.

[Contributed by Mrs. W. J. WHITFORD, Brookfield, N.Y.]

Materials: Barbour's white flax thread, No. 70, 3-cord, 200-yards spools, and 4 steel needles, No. 18 or No. 19.

Cast on 8 sts, 2 on 1st needle and 3 on each of 2 others.

1. K plain; each alternate row is also knit plain, hence will not be mentioned.

2. O, k 1, repeat.

4. O, k 2, repeat.

6. O, k 3, repeat.

8. O, k 4, repeat.

10. O, k 5, repeat.

12. O, k 6, repeat.

14. O, k 7, repeat.

16. O, sl and b, k 6, repeat.

18. O, k 1, o, sl, and b, k 5, repeat.

20. O, k 3, o, sl and b, k 4, repeat.

22. O, k 5, o, sl and b, k 3, repeat.

24. O, k 7, o, sl and b, k 2, repeat.

26. O, k 9, o, sl and b, k 1, repeat.

28. O, k 11, o, sl and b, repeat.

30. O, k 1, o, n, o, sl and b, k 9, repeat.

32. O, k 1, o, n, o, n, o, sl and b, k 8, repeat.

34. O, k 1, o, n, k 2, o, n, o, sl and b, k 7, repeat.

36. O, k 1, o, n, k 4, o, n, o, sl and b, k 6, repeat.

38. O, k 1, o, n, k 6, o, n, o, sl and b, k 5, repeat.

40. O, k 1, o, n, k 3, o, n, k 3, o, n, o, sl and b, k 4, repeat.

42. O, k 1, o, n, k 3, o, n, o, n, k 3, o, n, o, sl, and b, k 3, repeat.

44. O, k 1, o, n, k 3, o, n, o, n, o, n, k 3, o, n, o, sl and b, k 2, repeat.

46. O, k 1, o, n, k 3 (o, n), 4 times, k 3, o, n, o, sl and b, k 1, repeat.

48. O, k 1, o, n, k 3, o, n, o, n, k 2, o, n, o, n, k 3, o, n, o, sl and b, k 1, repeat.

50. O, k 1, o, n, k 3, o, n, o, n, k 4, o, n, o, n, k 3, o, n, sl and b, repeat.

52. O, n, repeat.

54. K 16, widen (by knitting the 1st loop of st in preceding row), repeat. You should now have 204 sts.

55 and 56. K plain.

57. O, n, repeat.

59. O, n, o, n, k 2, repeat.

61. K 1, slip it on needle last knit, then * o, n, o, n, k 2, repeat from *.

63. 65, and 67. Like 61st row.

69. O, n, repeat.

70, 71, 72, and 73. K plain. Hereafter let it be understood, as previously, that all rows not otherwise mentioned are knitted plain.

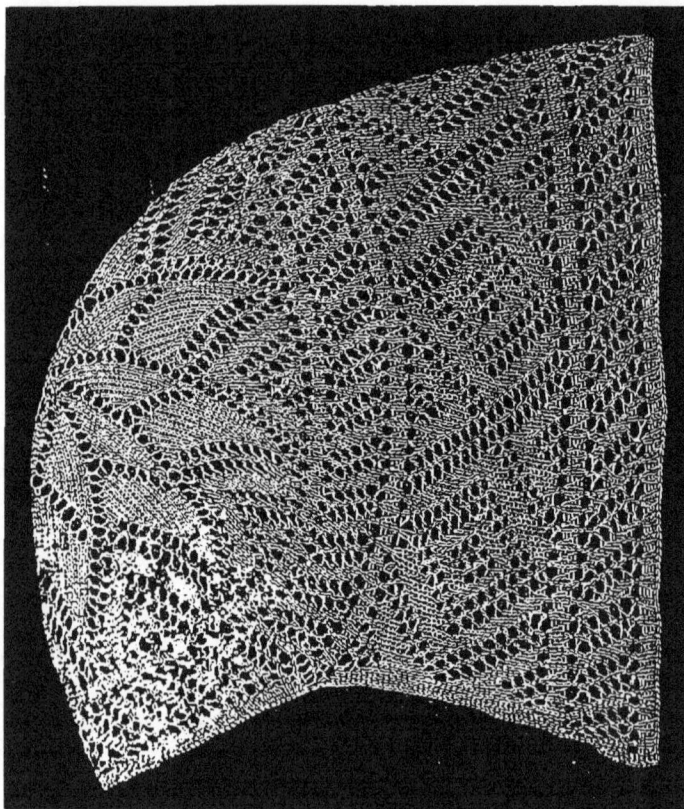

Body of Infant's Knitted Hood.

74. Bind off tightly 51 sts; then, retaining the last st on right-hand needle, o, n, repeat.

75. Purl every st. Alternate rows, not otherwise mentioned, will now be purled.

76. K 4, o, n, o, n, o, n, k 3, o, n, o, n, k 3, * o, n, k 3, o, n,

o, n, k 3, o, n, o, n, o, n, k 3, o, n, o, n, k 3, repeat from * 3 times, k 3, o, n, o, n, o, n, k 4.

78. K 5, * o, n, o, n, k 3, repeat; k 4.

80. K 6, * o, n, k 3, o, n, o, n, k 3, o, n, o, n, o, n, k 3, o, n, o, n, k 3, repeat from * 4 times, o, n, k 5.

82. K 10, * o, n, o, n, k 3 (o, n), 4 times, k 3, o, n, o, n, k 6, repeat; k 3.

84. K 9, * o, n, o, n, k 3, o, n, o, n, k 2, o, n, o, n, k 3, o, n, o, n, k 4, repeat; k 4.

86. K 8, * o, n, o, n, k 3, o, n, o, n, k 4, o, n, o, n, k 3, o, n, o, n, k 2, repeat; k 4.

88. K 7, o, n, o, n, * k 3, o, n, o, n, k 2, o, n, k 2, o, n, o, n, k 3 (o, n), 4 times, repeat 3 times from *, k 3, o, n, o, n, k 2, o, n, k 2, o, n, o, n, k 3, o, n, o, n, k 6.

90. K 6, o, n, o, n, * k 3, o, n, o, n, k 2, o, n, o, n, k 2, o, n, o, n, k 3, o, n, o, n, o, n, repeat 3 times, k 3, o, n, o, n, k 2, o, n, o, n, k 2, o, n, o, n, k 3, o, n, o, n, k 5.

92. K 5, o, n, o, n, * k 3, o, n, o, n, k 2, o, n, o, n, o, n, k 2, o, n, o, n, k 3, o, n, o, n, repeat 3 times, k 3, o, n, o, n, k 2, o, n, o, n, o, n, k 2, o, n, o, n, k 3, o, n, o, n, k 4.

94. Like 90th.

96. Like 88th.

98. Like 86th.

100. Like 84th.

102. Like 82d.

104. Like 80th.

106. Like 78th.

108. Like 76th.

110. O, n, repeat.

112 and 114. Plain.

116. Like 110th.

118. K 1, * o, n, o, n, k 2, repeat.

120. K 2, * o, n, o, n, k 2, repeat.

122. K 3, * o, n, o, n, k 2, repeat.

124. K 4, * o, n, o, n, k 2, repeat.

126. K 1, o, n, k 2, * o, n, o, n, k 2, repeat.

128. O, n, repeat.

130 and **131.** Plain.

134. Bind off.

This completes the body of hood. For a border knit an edge, using 2 needles:

Cast on 13 sts.

1. Sl 1, k 1, o,n, k 3, n, o, n, o, k 1, o, k 1.

2. K plain, purling the "over" loops; all other alternate rows the same.

3. Sl 1, k 1, o, n, k 2, n, o, n, o, k 3, o, k 1.

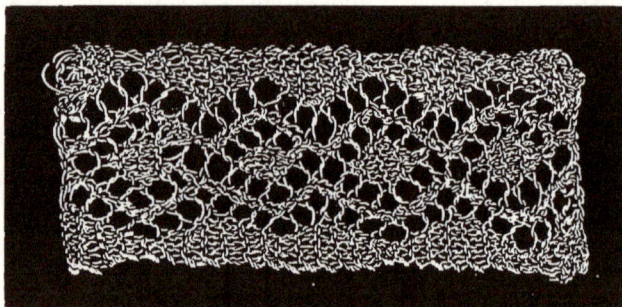

Insertion for Knitted Hood.

5. Sl 1, k 1, o, n, k 1, n, o, n, o, k 5, o, k 1.

7. Sl 1, k 1, o, n, k 3, o, n, o, n, k 1, n, o, n.

9. Sl 1, k 1, o, n, k 4, o, n, o, k 3 tog, o, n.

11. Sl 1, k 1, o, n, k 5, o, k 3 tog, o, n.

12. Plain. Repeat from 1st row.

This edge is to be sewed all around the bonnet, over and over. If more ornamentation is desired, add bows or a fan of lace on top of bonnet, made by sewing the edge on either side of an insertion, made as follows:

Cast on 15 sts.

1. K 4, n, o, n, o, n, o, k 5.

2. K plain, purling loops ; alternate rows same.
3. K 3, n, o, n, o, k 1, o, n, o, n, k 3.
5. K 2, n, o, n, o, k 3, o, n, o, n, k 2.
7. K 1, n, o, n, o, k 5, o, n, o, n, k 1.
9. K 3, o, n, o, n, k 1, n, o, n, o, k 3.
11. K 4, o, n, o, k 3 tog, o, n, o, k 4.
13. K 5, o, k 3 tog, o, n, o, k 5.
14. K plain ; repeat from 1st row.

This little hood or bonnet should be lined with silk, with ribbon ties, and loops among the lace bows, to match the lining silk in

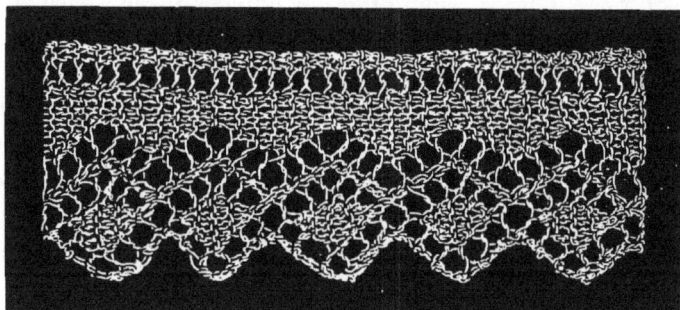

Border for Knitted Hood.

color ; it will be found very dainty. It may be made larger if desired, by knitting the 16th row like the 14th, with 8 plain sts, etc., thus making the star larger and enlarging the whole pattern. More rows may also be put in the border, like the 59th row. This design is nearly all original with the writer, who has made the little hoods in different sizes, the larger being more elaborate.

After 74th row the bonnet is knitted in rows, back and forth, and 1 needle may be dispensed with. The insertion may be made wider, if desired, by casting on 4 more stitches and knitting 2 plain on each edge before doing the fancy part.

WIDE TATTED LACE.

FIRST PRIZE ARTICLE.

[Contributed by Mrs. J. M. HOBKON, New York City, N.Y.]

Use Barbour's flax thread, white, No. 80, 3-cord, 200-yards spools.

Begin in the centre of rosette with a ring of * 2 dk, 1 p, repeat till you have 12 p, close ring, break and fasten thread. The outside row of rings is made with 1 thread; beginning with a small ring, make 2 dk, 1 p, 2 dk, join to p of middle ring, 2 dk, 1 p, 2 dk, close. Then the next outer ring, 4 dk, 1 p, 4 dk, 1 p, 4 dk, 1 p, 4 dk, close; small ring, 2 dk, join to side p of previous small ring, 2 dk, join to centre ring, 2 dk, 1 p, 2 dk, close; then the next outer ring, 4 dk, join to previous ring, 4 dk, 1 p, 4 dk, 1 p, 4 dk. Continue in this way until there are 12 rings of each size, joining first to last; break and fasten thread.

Make as many of these rosettes as desired, according to the quantity of trimming wanted, allowing 6 for each point after the first; 2 of these should be joined together in working by the centre picots of 2 successive large rings, then 2 more in the same way, and a 3d between these 2, by next rings of each below the side joinings, to 4 successive rings of the 3d rosette. The 6th rosette forms centre of square.

The square is made with 2 threads. Make a ring of 4 dk, 1 p, 4 dk, 1 p, 4 dk, 1 p, 4 dk, close; with 2 threads, a scallop of 4 dk, 1 p, 4 dk. At the corners of the square a ring is omitted. The sample shows the method of joining so plainly, and the whole design is so simple, that it seems almost unnecessary to take space for entire details. The small rosettes connecting the points with the 2 upper and larger rosettes consist simply of 5 rings, made with 1 thread, exactly like the outer rings of large rosettes. The heading is formed of 2 rows of rings and scallops, made the same as for the square; that is, a ring of 4 dk, 1 p, 4 dk, 1 p, 4 dk, 1 p, 4 dk,

Wide Tatted Lace.

close; with 2 threads, 4 dk, 1 p, 4 dk. Every ring after the 1st is of course joined to the preceding one by side p, and in making the upper row each ring is joined in working to the centre p of ring below. The p of 2 successive scallops is joined to rosette, then 4 scallops without joining, then 2 are joined to corner of square.

This design developed in coarser thread, or in the colored flosses, is lovely as a finish for table-scarfs and other similar decorations.

TATTED BORDER, WITH CORNER.

SECOND PRIZE ARTICLE.

[Contributed by JENNIE R. WELCH, Lawrence, Kan.]

This border, of which the illustration shows one-quarter, is suitable for handkerchiefs, cushion-squares, etc., and is worked with Barbour's flax thread, white, No. 60, 3-cord, 200-yards spools. For very fine work, use No. 80 or even No. 100.

1. The border is made with 1 and 2 threads, as follows: Begin with the 3-leaved figures, joined by scallops on the inner edge ; tie the working threads together ; * using but 1 thread, make a ring of 2 dk (double knots), and 7 times, alternately, 1 picot, 2 dk, close ; work 2 more similar rings close to this.   After working the 3d ring, fasten to the 1st ring where closed, turn the work upside down, take the thread from the other shuttle, carry it around the hand for the hand-thread, and with the shuttle used for the rings work a scallop of 2 dk, and 7 times, alternately, 1 p, 2 dk. Turn the work back again, and repeat from *.   The 3-leaved figures, however, must be joined to each other by the middle p of each outer leaf.   The corner must be formed in this as in the following rounds ; to form the corner, join the figures by the middle p of the 2 centre leaves instead of the outer ones.

2. Tie threads together ; * work, first, with 1 thread, a ring of 1 dk, 4 times, alternately, 1 p, 2 dk, join to the middle p of a scallop of preceding row, 4 times, alternately, 2 dk, 1 p, then 1 dk, close the ring, turn the work, and close to this ring, with both threads, work a scallop of 2 dk, and 7 times, alternately, 1 p, 2 dk, turn the work, and repeat from * until the corner is reached, where the scallop should have 11 p, separated by 2 dk ; 1 ring joins the 3d p of the corner scallop of preceding row, the next the 6th p of same scallop.   Then proceed as before.

3. This row is composed of 3-leaved figures and scallops, like the

1st row. In forming the corners, 3 of the 3-leaved figures are joined to the corner scallop of previous row, the 1st to 2d p, 2d to 6th p, and 3d to 10th p, the 2d figure not being joined to 1st and 3d.

4. Now follows a round of rosettes, worked as follows: With 1 thread work a ring of 1 dk, 1 p, 2 dk, 1 p; repeat until you have 8

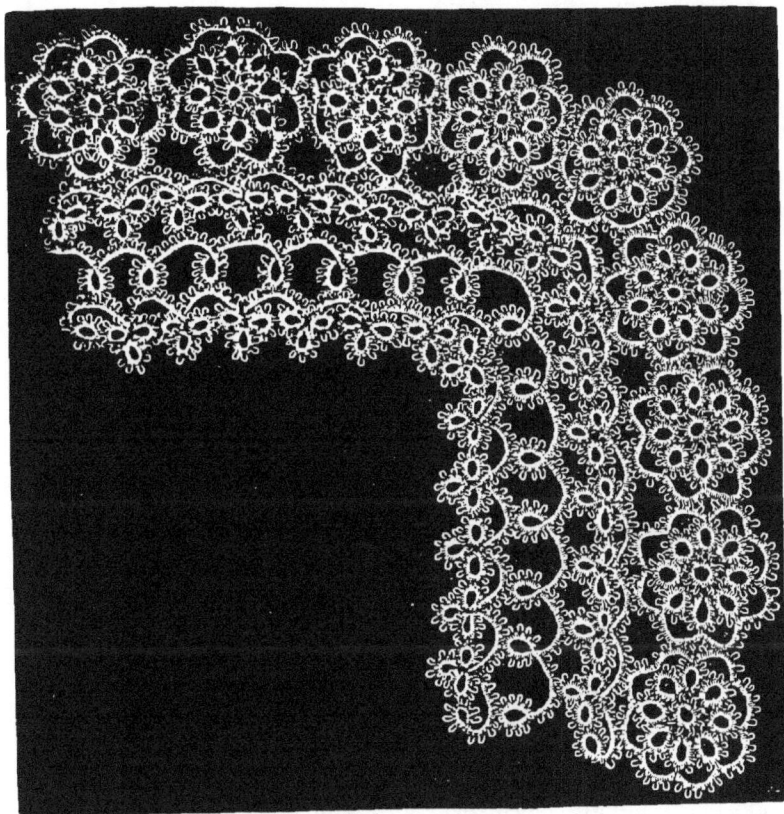

Tatted Border, with Corner.

p with 2 lk between each, 1 dk, close. Join the thread to the 1st p, and work a ring as follows, leaving a very short space of thread: 4 dk, 1 p, * 2 dk, 1 p, repeat from * until you have 7 p, then 4 dk, close; join thread in next p of middle ring, 4 dk, join to last p of preceding ring, * 2 dk, 1 p, repeat from * to form 6 p, 4 dk, close. Repeat until you have 8 rings around the middle ring, and join last ring to 1st. For the outer scallops use both threads. Join to the middle p of a ring, * 2 dk, 5 times, alternately, 1 p, 2 dk, join to middle p of next ring, and repeat from * all around. Join the rosettes to the scallops of the preceding round, as you work, by the middle p of each 2 scallops, except the corner rosette, which must be joined between 2 scallops of preceding row. The rosettes join each other by middle p of 2 corresponding scallops on each.

These rosettes make a very pretty cover for toilet-cushion, or may be combined in a pretty lace.

TATTED EDGE.

[Contributed by Mrs. J. M. HOBSON, New York, N.Y.]

Use Barbour's flax thread, 3-cord, 200-yards spools, No. 25, and 2 shuttles.

The 3 large loops, forming the clover leaf, are made first. The side loops contain 5 dk, 1 p, 5 dk, 1 p, 5 dk, 1 p, 5 dk; the middle

Tatted Edge.

loop, in order to elongate it a little, contains an extra dk on each side of the middle picot. Tie on the 2d thread and make 5 knots; make the small loops, containing each 2 dk, 1 p, 2 dk, 1 p, 2 dk, 1 p, 2 dk, with first thread; then, using both threads, form the unclosed loop of 5 dk, 1 p, 5 dk, 1 p, 5 dk, attaching to middle p of upper small loop; then make a similar unclosed loop before making next 2 small loops, for which always use the first thread.

TATTED STAR.

[Contributed by Miss JENNIE R. WELCH, Lawrence, Kan.]

This star is worked with Barbour's flax thread, white or cream, No. 50, 3-cord, 200-yards spools.

1. Begin in the centre with 1 thread; make 1 dk, 10 p, separated each by 2 dk, 1 dk, fasten thread and cut off.

2. With 2 threads make a round of scallops, join to 1 p in ring just made, * 4 dk, 1 p, 4 dk, 1 p, 4 dk, miss 1 p of middle ring, join to next, and repeat from * until 5 scallops are worked. Fasten thread and cut off.

3. This round is also worked with 2 threads. * Join to 1st p of scallop of previous round, 2 dk, 7 p, separated by 2 dk, 2 dk, join to next p of same scallop, 2 dk, 3 p, separated each by 2 dk, 2 dk; repeat from *.

4. * With 1 thread only, work a ring of 2 dk, 4 p, each separated by 2 dk, 2 dk, join to middle p of

Tatted Star.

one of the larger scallops of previous round, 2 dk, 4 p, each separated by 2 dk, 2 dk, turn the work, and with 2 threads make a scallop of 2 dk, 13 p, each separated by 2 dk, 2 dk, turn work again, and with 1 thread work a ring of 4 dk, 9 p, separated by 2 dk, 4 dk, close, work another ring close to this of 4 dk, join to last p of previous ring,

2 dk, 4 p, each separated by 2 dk, join to the middle p of next
small scallop of previous round, 2 dk, 4 p, each separated by 2 dk,
4 dk; now, a 3d ring similar to 1st, only that instead of forming
the 1st p, join to the last p of the preceding ring, turn the work,
and with both threads work 1 scallop like the preceding. Repeat
from *.

5. * With 1 thread only work a ring of 2 dk, 7 p, each separated
by 2 dk, 2 dk, turn work; work another ring of 2 dk, 3 p, each separated by 2 dk, 2 dk, join to middle p of scallop of previous round,
2 dk, 3 p, each separated by 2 dk, fasten the rings where the sts
are closed, and with both threads, without turning the work, work a
scallop of 2 dk, 7 p, each separated by 2 dk, 2 dk, join to the 4th
following p, 1 scallop of 2 dk, 3 p, each separated by 2 dk, 2 dk,
join to 3d p of next scallop of previous round, then 1 scallop of 2 dk,
7 p, each separated by 2 dk, 2 dk.   Repeat from *.

This star is very desirable for cushion-covers and a variety of
purposes, and the small centre star may be used for joining the
larger ones.

TATTED EDGE.

[Contributed by Miss ELLEN M. BRUCE, Tallapoosa, Ga.]

This edge is made with 2 shuttles and in 3 rows. Make lower row
first.   Sample shown was made with No. 35, 3-cord, 200-yards
spools, Barbour's flax thread.   Fill both shuttles and fasten ends of
shuttle threads together.

1.   With 1 shuttle make a ring of 3 dk, 1 p, 3 dk, 1 p, 3 dk, 1 p,
3 dk (according to full instructions given in No. 1, Barbour's Prize
Series); this ring and all others made should be fastened so that when
the edging is stretched the ring will not pull apart.   To do this, with
a crochet-needle draw the thread under the ring where the knots
meet to form the circle, through the loop formed by doing this pass
the shuttle, then draw thread tight.   Now turn the ring so that the
middle picot will be downward, pass thread from the other shuttle

over the hand, winding around little finger, for hand thread, and
with the same shuttle used for ring make * 3 dk, 1 p, 3 dk, join to
last p of ring just made, again using the 2 shuttles, make 3 dk, 1 p,
3 dk. With shuttle used to make 1st ring (which for convenience
we will call ring thread) make 3 dk, join to middle p of 1st ring, 6
dk, 1 p, 6 dk, 1 p, 3 dk, fasten; with 2 shuttles make 3 dk, 1 p, 3
dk ; with ring thread make 3 dk, join to last p of previous ring, 3 dk,
1 p, 3 dk, 1 p, 3 dk, 1 p, 3 dk, 1 p, 3 dk, 1 p, 3 dk, 1 p, 3 dk;
fasten; with 2 shuttles make 3 dk, 1 p, 3 dk, and with ring thread 3
dk, join to last p of previous ring, * 3 dk, 1 p, repeat from last * 7

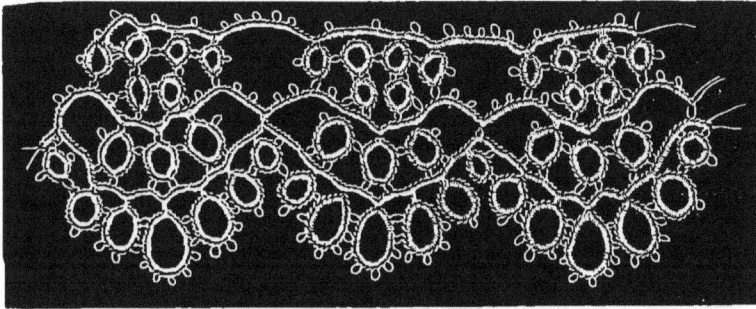

Tatted Edge.

times, 3 dk, fasten ; with 2 shuttles make 3 dk, 1 p, 3 dk ; with ring
thread, 3 dk, join to last p of previous ring, * 3 dk, 1 p, repeat from
last * 5 times, 3 dk, fasten ; with 2 shuttles, 3 dk, 1 p, 3 dk ; with
ring thread, 3 dk, join to last p of previous ring, 6 dk, 1 p, 6 dk, 1 p,
3 dk, fasten ; with 2 shuttles, 3 dk, 1 p, 3 dk with ring thread, 3 dk,
join to last p of previous ring, 3 dk, 1 p, 3 dk, 1 p, 3 dk. Repeat
from 1st *.

2. Join thread from both shuttles together, join 1 thread to middle
p of 1st group of 3 dk, 1 p, 3 dk made with 2 shuttles, in previous
row ; * with 2 shuttles make 3 dk, 1 p, 3 dk, 1 p, 3 dk, 1 p, 3 dk,
1 p, 3 dk; with ring thread make 3 dk, 1 p, 5 dk, join to p in middle of 2d group of 3 dk, 1 p, 3 dk, of previous row, 2 dk, join to
middle p of 3d group, 5 dk, 1 p, 3 dk, fasten (for convenience,

call this ring No. 1) ; with 2 shuttles make 3 dk ; now with upper
thread make ring of 3 dk, 1 p, 3 dk, 1 p, 3 dk, 1 p, 3 dk, fasten ;
with 2 shuttles make 3 dk ; with ring thread make 3 dk, join to last
p in ring No. 1, 5 dk, join to p in middle of 4th group, 2 dk, join to
middle p of 5th group, 5 dk, 1 p, 3 dk fasten (call this ring No. 2) ;
with 2 shuttles make 3 dk, with the upper thread, 3 dk, join to last
p of small ring, 3 dk, 1 p, 3 dk, 1 p, 3 dk, fasten ; with 2 shuttles,
3 dk ; with ring thread, 3 dk, join to last p of ring No. 2, 5 dk, join
to middle p of 6th group, 2 dk, join to middle p of 7th group, 5 dk,
1 p, 3 dk, fasten ; with 2 shuttles make 3 dk, 1 p, 3 dk, 1 p, 3 dk,
1 p, 3 dk, 1 p, 3 dk, join to middle p of 8th group. Repeat from *.

3.   Join threads from both shuttles ; * with ring thread make 3 dk,
1 p, 3 dk, join to third p in long group made with 2 shuttles in previous row, 3 dk, 1 p, 3 dk, fasten (call this ring A) ; with 2 shuttles
make 3 dk, 1 p, 3 dk ; with ring thread 3 dk, join to last p of ring A,
3 dk, join to middle p of small ring in row below, 3 dk, 1 p, 3 dk,
fasten (call this ring B) ; with 2 shuttles make 3 dk, 1 p, 3 dk ;
with ring thread 3 dk, join to last p of ring B, 3 dk, join to middle
p of ring in row below, 3 dk, 1 p, 3 dk, fasten (call this ring C) ;
with 2 shuttles 3 dk, 1 p, 3 dk, with ring thread 3 dk, join to last p
of ring C, 3 dk, join to 2d p of long group below, 3 dk, 1 p, 3 dk,
fasten ; with 2 shuttles, 3 dk, 1 p, 3 dk, 1 p, 3 dk, 1 p, 3 dk, 1 p, 3
dk, 1 p, 3 dk.

Repeat from *.   This is more tedious in detail than in working.

DEPARTMENT 6.—BOOK 1.

COLORED ANTIQUE LACE.

FIRST PRIZE ARTICLE.

[Contributed by Miss A. M. FITCH, New Haven, Conn.]

This is worked on a netted foundation, made from directions for "square-mesh" netting on page 57 of Barbour's Prize Series, No. 1. It is 34 squares wide (33 squares when finished, as 1 mesh is cut off when buttonholed, to make a nice edge), and may be netted of No. 25 or No. 40 Barbour's flax thread, 3-cord, 200-yards spools, with larger or smaller size of mesh, according to the use that is to be made of the work. The sample is netted of No. 40, écru flax thread, with a mesh about ¼ inch wide. To give it a still deeper tint, and also to stiffen it slightly, the netting is wet in boiled starch made of coffee. When dry, stretch in a frame for convenience in working. The sample shown is designed for the end of a silk pongee table-scarf.

After completing the netted foundation, the leaves and the row of squares around the scallops are darned in with the same No. flax thread as the netting (No. 40), beginning with the squares in 8th mesh from the bottom, darning 2 squares, then descending 1 square with each row (4 squares), darning 4 in a row for bottom of scallop, ascending 4, darning 2 in a row, etc. Leave a plain row of squares, that is, without filling, on each side of the darned row, filling in with the festoon-stitch, which is one of the simplest and most effective known, the row of squares below the plain one, and next to the edge. After darning in the leaves, the size of which can readily be shown by counting the squares around them, the whole remaining netting is worked with festoon-stitch, or "point d'esprit,"

in rows, forward and back, the thread crossing over and under so
that the mesh thread comes between, on each side of square, with
the mesh knot in the centre of the circle thus formed. With a little
practice it is very easy. This filling-in stitch is worked with No. 70
Barbour's flax thread, 3-cord, 200-yards spools. This is cut in
convenient lengths for working, loosely braided, and wet in coffee to
tint it like the foundation. The outlining of the leaves, the border,
stars, etc., are worked with Barbour's flax embroidery threads, size 0,
in four art shades, olive, red, yellow, and blue. The veining of the
leaves and the stems may also be done in the embroidery threads,

Antique or Oriental Lace.

but an even more decided Oriental effect is given the work by using
a little copper and gold tinsel cord for the latter. The 1st star in
upper right-hand corner is of red, the star below, in lower right-
hand corner, is blue, the darned circle following, red, the 2d star of
yellow, the two small circles connected with the leaf above are
blue, and the leaf is outlined with green, run in around the edge of
darning, being caught under a thread now and then. The 2d leaf
is outlined with red, the upper star being yellow, and the lower one
blue, while the small circle a little to the right and below the blue
star is of green. The 3d circle is red, the star in the lower left-hand

corner yellow, the one above blue, and the 3d leaf outlined with green. Of the 4 threads run in the top, the lower one is yellow, the 2d blue, 3d green, and 4th, or upper thread, red. The threads above the row of darned squares are, 1st, blue (next the squares), and 2d, yellow, with several cross stitches above the squares darned in a row. Below, 1st thread is green, and 2d or lower one red, with cross-stitches below the horizontal squares.

After the work is complete, buttonhole-stitch across 2 squares, where 2 squares are darned, descend 4, then work across 4 squares, ascend 4, etc. Buttonhole-stitch the ends, also.

The same design may be worked on a netting of No. 25 flax thread, with large mesh, making a very effective mantel valance or lambrequin, covering the shelf with natural-color silk pongee. The same design of leaves arranged on a square of netting makes a very handsome sofa cushion, covering the pillow with pongee, and finishing with an edging fulled at the corners. The lower part of this design is a very good pattern for an edging to be used in many ways. For the expense involved, this makes a very beautiful piece of work.

Netting may be made of use in many ways. A handsome towel, which may be utilized as a "sham" for the rack, is made of one and one-fourth yards of fine huckabuck towelling, with netted border and fringe. To make it, even the huckaback at both ends, and turn a hem of 3 inches, finishing at the top with any simple drawn-work pattern, which may be worked with the same No. of flax thread used in netting the fringe. Buttonhole-stitch the edge of hem, putting the stitches about one-fourth inch apart, and net into the button-holing according to the directions given for diamond-netting, in Book No. 1, page 57, using the white flax thread, No. 25, 3-cord, 200-yards spools, and making the border 10 meshes deep; tie in each loop a fringe made of same thread. Above the hem and drawn-work border, in middle of towel, work a large initial letter, using white embroidery flax thread, size oo; this may be either worked solidly or outlined.

A pretty cushion cover or doily may be netted of Barbour's white flax thread, No. 40, 3-cord, 200-yards spools, 42 ¼-inch meshes square, with a border of the diamond-mesh netting 8 or 9 meshes wide, slightly fulled.   Any pattern used for cross-stitch embroidery may be copied for darning in.   That used for the doily in question was very simple, one row of squares being left around the edge.   With Barbour's linen floss, size aa, darn over and under 2 squares, the threads crossing above and under the centre thread ; repeat this around the edge, next row to outside row, missing 1 square between each 2 that are darned ; miss 2 rows of squares, and darn another row in the same way, then darn, horizontally, over the 2d and 3d squares of the 4 between.   This will make a figure with four squares in the centre.   In the corners, make an additional square, and in the centre make 5 squares, darned around in the same way.   Very simple and pretty.

In cut-work Barbour's flax threads are invaluable.   Having a suitable pattern stamped on linen, begin by buttonholing the stamped linen with a close buttonhole, using flax thread, size oo, or spool thread, No. 40, using the latter always for single-thread lines stamped in the pattern.   When all is worked, cut the linen from the edge and throughout the pattern, close to the outer edge of the buttonholing. This is very pretty, not only for all articles in linen, but also on felt or chamois, buttonholed in colored flax threads, making the dainty lamp-mats, and mats for rose-bowls now so much used.

NETTED DRAPE FOR CHAIR.

SECOND PRIZE ARTICLE.

[Contributed by Mrs. JOHN SHAW, Red Oak, Iowa.]

Materials : Barbour's linen floss, A, and flax thread, No. 40, 3-cord, 200-yards spools.

Fill a netting-needle with the floss, and with No. 11 mesh cast on 55 loops.

1. Net 2 in each loop.

2 and 3. With the No. 40 flax thread and No. 4 mesh, net plain.

4. Plain, with floss and No. 11 mesh.

5. Net 3 loops together to end of row.

6. Plain.

7. Net 3 in each loop.

8 and 9. Same as 2d and 3d rows.

10. Plain, with floss and mesh No. 11.

This completes one open stripe. For the checked stripe, work with the No. 40 linen and mesh No. 4.

1. Net 1, * net 1, putting thread once around mesh and netting 2 loops together, net 1, net 2 together: repeat. The last loop will be that having the thread around the mesh.

2. Net 1, 2d st not to be netted close to mesh but up to loop, 3d st to be a small one drawn close to mesh, then draw out the mesh, put it into the last long loop, and repeat.

3. Net 2, net 1 up to loop, repeat.

4. Net 2, net 1, put linen around mesh, repeat.

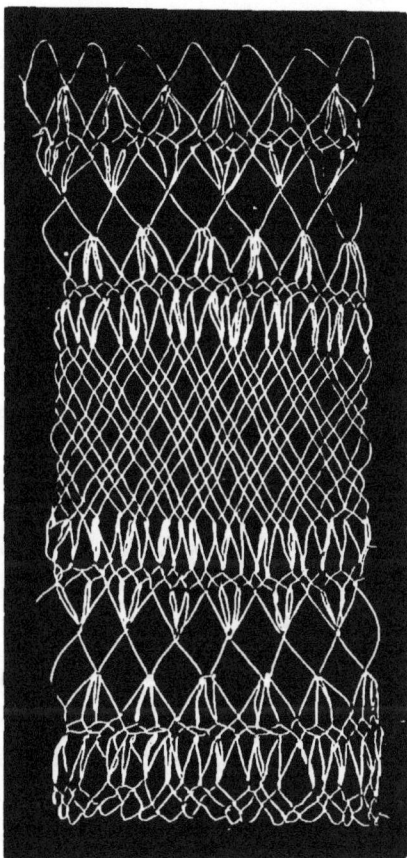

Netted Drape.

5. Net 1, putting linen around mesh, net 1, * draw out mesh, net 1, net 1 up to loop, next st to be small and netted close to mesh, repeat from *.

6. Net 1, putting linen around mesh, draw out mesh, * net 2, net 1 up to loop, repeat from *.

This finishes one pattern. Work two more patterns the same, except that the 1st row is not decreased, but done thus : net 1, * net 1, putting linen around mesh once, net 2, repeat from *.

Open stripe :

1. With the floss and mesh No. 11, net 1, net 2 in next loop, * net 1, net 2 in each of next 2 loops, repeat from * to end of row.

Repeat from 2d and 3d rows of 1st open stripe to complete the drape. Three open and 2 checked stripes are required. Finish the last open stripe by netting a row, working 2 loops together. Add fringe for a finish. Rows of ribbon may be run in the open spaces, if fancied.

The No. 11 mesh is about ¾ inch, and No. 4, ¼ inch.

NETTED GUIPURE BALLOON LACE.

[Contributed by Mrs. ANDREW J. SUMNER, East Middlebury, Vt.]

Materials : Barbour's flax thread, écru, 3-cord, 200-yards spools, No. 40, a long steel netting-needle, and a bone mesh less than ¼ inch wide.

The heading of the design is first netted in a long strip 5 meshes wide, in diamond-netting, described and illustrated in Barbour's Prize Series, No. 1. A row of diamonds is then darned in with the same thread, using an ordinary needle, and passing the thread over, under, and around, covering 4 meshes. Then a sufficient length of the netting is gathered on a string and either pinned to a lead cushion or by a strap crossed over the foot, and the netted border done thus :

1. With the thread twice over the needle, or with a large mesh, net 6 sts in each diamond.

2 and 3. Once over the small mesh, such as was used for the diamond-netting first made, in each st.

4. Use wide mesh, like 1st row.

5. Gather the loops into 1 st, netting with the wide mesh.

When washed and starched push each group out into balloon

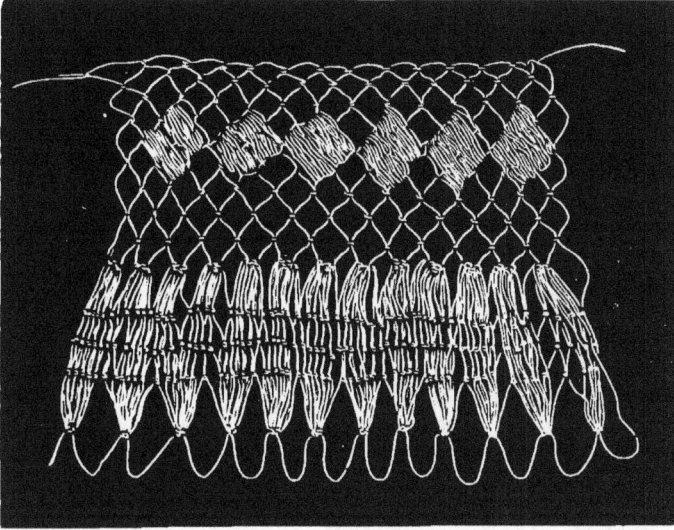

Netted Guipure Balloon Lace.

shape. Very pretty trimming for wash dresses, and for a variety of purposes. It is very durable, made in the flax thread, lasting for many years.

ANTIQUE VALANCE FOR CLOVER-LEAF TABLE.

[Contributed by Mrs. J. E. BURGESS, Madison, Wis.]

Barbour's carpet thread, or No. 16, 3-cord, flax thread, in balls ½ inch mesh, and large netting-needle.

Antique Valance for Clover-Leaf Table.

Make a strip of square-mesh netting, 30 squares deep, and long enough to extend around table. If the ball thread is used, dip in thin starch made with boiled coffee. The work can be done more evenly in a frame, but is not difficult, save to describe. It can be easily taken from the sample. The edge is buttonholed, and the outside squares cut away.

The table itself is so quickly and inexpensively made that I am sure the ladies will all enjoy having one. Those who are possessed of some mechanical genius will not even need the services of a carpenter. The top is sawed out in three deep scallops, to represent a clover-leaf, and there are three legs, each supporting a leaf, and crossing in the middle. These may be turned, or broom-sticks which are past service as such, used. Having used more than one hundred spools of Barbour's flax thread for antique bedspread and shams, I gave the empty reels to a lady who utilized them in making the legs of a clover-leaf table, running wire rods through them. The top of table should be covered with four or five thicknesses of wadding, and over that any chosen material. I used yellow figured damask, putting a tack in centre of table, and one in centre of each leaf to hold the covering firmly while tacking to the edge, afterwards removing them. The valance I lined with yellow satin, of the same shade as the top covering, nailing it on with brass tacks. I put three small balls on each point, and a big bow of yellow ribbon (all matching the satin lining) on one side. It is the prettiest thing in my room, and universally admired.

GUIPURE LACE.

[Contributed by Miss SUSAN H. MANN, Greenfield, Mass.]

Materials: a strip of embroidery crash or butcher's linen, for foundation, and Barbour's flax thread, No. 60, 3-cord, 200-yards spools, for working the stitches.

Take a strip of the linen 3 inches wide. Beginning a half-inch from the edge, draw 12 threads the length of the strip, leave 3

threads, draw 12 more, and proceed in this way until you have 7
drawn spaces, leaving 3 threads between each.

Then draw the short way, a few threads at a time, as you work,
drawing 12 and leaving 3, as before, being careful not to draw
through the plain part at top and bottom.   Overcast all the loose
threads with No. 100 spool flax thread, and buttonhole-stitch over

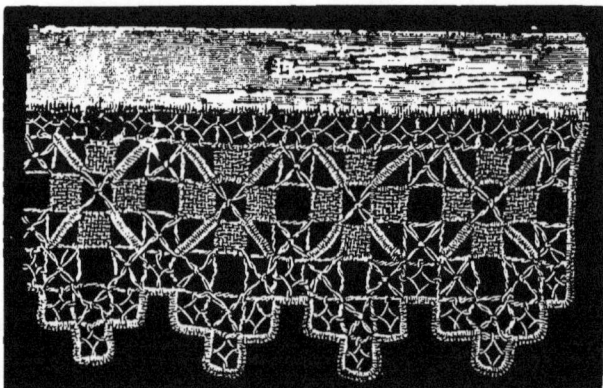

Guipure Lace.

2 threads across the top, next to the lace, and around the points.
After the work is done the linen is to be cut away.

The crash must be put in a frame, such as is described on page
56, Barbour's Prize Series, No. 1, in order to keep it straight while
working.   The stitches given in this model are very simple, and can
be easily worked from the illustration.

Any of the antique or guipure lace patterns can be made in this
way by those who find it difficult to make the netted foundation.

DARNED NET LACE.

FIRST PRIZE ARTICLE.

[Contributed by Mrs. HARRIET NICKLIN, New Castle, Pa.]

Materials : Barbour's flax embroidery thread, white, size 8, brussels net, linen thread, finest possible to get, and lace picots for edging.

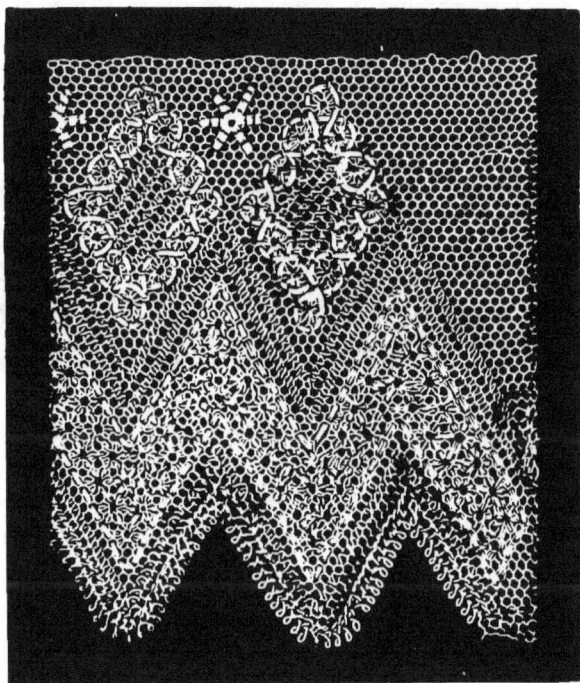

Darned Net Lace.

The work is done on the net, at least 3 inches wide. The deep points outlined with the embroidery thread are first worked, then

the space between is darned in with the fine linen in tiny wheels,
worked around a mesh of the lace, by starting from the centre and
darning over the surrounding 6 meshes. Then begin on the next
nearest mesh. There are 8 in depth of these wee circles in a point,
and two rows of them. Outline these points with the linen floss,
which has a gloss like silk, then below the points, using again the
very fine linen, work over 1 mesh of the lace, exactly following
the points, leaving 1 row of meshes above and below. Repeat
above the points, working in a double row with a row of meshes
between.

Now select a mesh exactly in the centre of the last rows done, and
work around it 6 times, as at first between the points. This is the

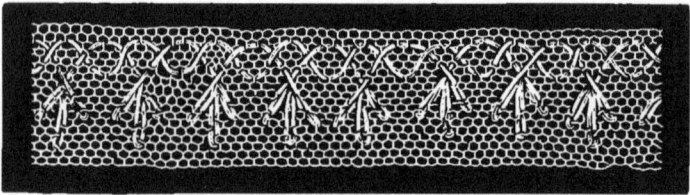

Darned Net Insertion.

lowest circle of the diamond above; follow the weave of the lace
for the other circles. Twelve of these make an exact diamond. Fill
in the centre of these diamonds, diagonally, working over 1 mesh of
the lace net, the same as in the long rows; 4 rows fill the centre.
Then outline with the linen floss, crossing above and below each
circle.

Darn the 6-pointed stars with the fine linen.

When the thread is nearly used out of the needle, tie a sailor's
knot instead of fastening the thread and commencing again.

Lace picots finish the edge, and the picots must be sewed a stitch
in every mesh, leaving 1 row of meshes between it and the work.
When sewed firmly and evenly, with a pair of sharp scissors cut the
lace away from under the picots, leaving the edge in points.

This is a very lovely pattern for edging handkerchiefs, for collars, ties, chemisettes, or any article that requires fine, delicate lace. The insertion given, darned entirely with the flax embroidery thread, may be combined with it in many ways. Some may prefer to omit the darning with fine linen, substituting for the rows of wheels in the points a pattern similar to that which outlines the diamonds. The 6-pointed star is also prettily darned in with the floss.

The lace chosen to work upon should be rather fine, as it makes the points sharper.

GRAPE-LEAF DOILY.

SECOND PRIZE ARTICLE.

[Contributed by Mrs. HENRY KRIEGER, Orenada, Powers Co., Col.]

Materials: Barbour's flax thread, No. 40, 3-cord, 200-yards spools, steel crochet hook, and lace net of rather large mesh.

1. Ch 25, 2 dc in last 2 sts, ch 22, 1 dc in 1st of 25 ch; this is for the smallest part of leaf; for the 2d part, ch 30, 2 dc in last sts 2, ch 28, 1 dc in 1st st; for the 3d and largest part of leaf, ch 40, 2 dc in last 2 sts, close this part also with 1 sc in 1st of 40 ch; repeat the 2d and then the 1st part of leaf, and close leaf with 1 dc.

2. Work around the whole leaf in dc, 1 dc in every st of ch except 1st and last in every section; in the point of each leaf make 3 dc in a st, in order to prevent curling. Work 2 more rows in this way, missing 2 and 3 sts on the inner part of each section, where they come together, so that they will fit smoothly.

3. Ch 5, miss 1, 1 dc in next, repeat all around, not going down between the sections where they touch, but drawing them together.

The grapes are begun in the middle with 4 ch; join, work 2 dc in each st; continue working around and widening to make the work lie flat, putting hook through both loops of sts. From 4 to 6 rounds should be made. Join the grapes to each other and to the leaf sections by sl st when working. There are 6 grapes in each cluster, fastened between 1st and 2d sections on one side, and between 2d and 3d sections on the other side.

For the tendril, fasten between 2d and 3d sections, make a ch of 85 sts, turn; make 1 dc over every ch, form in loops, and join either with sc, or needle and thread, to the leaf. On the opposite side, between 1st and 2d sections, make another tendril, smaller, but in much the same way. For the loops at top, fasten in at intersection, ch 28, turn, 1 dc in each st, turn, 1 dc in each dc of last row,

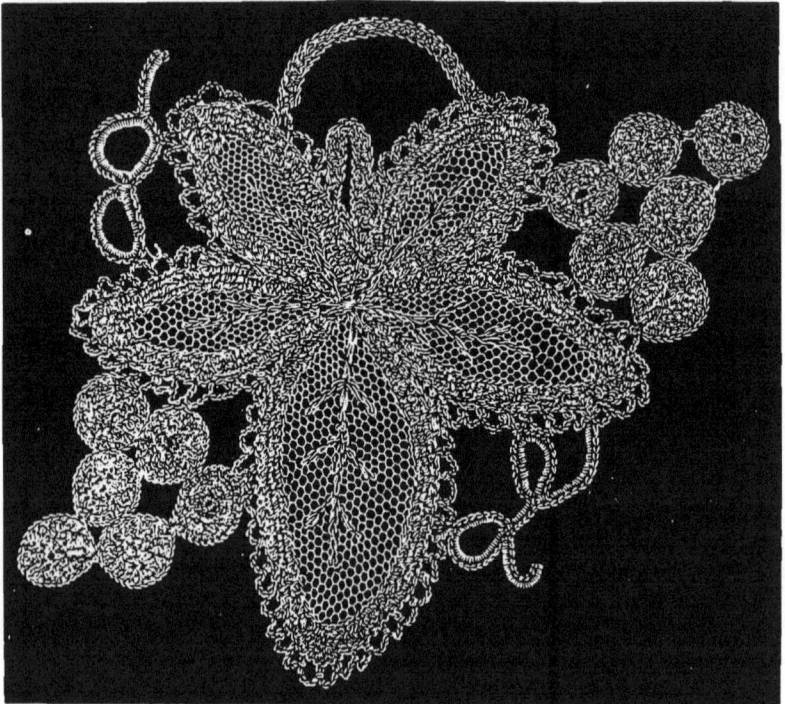

Grape-Leaf Doily.

and fasten in 2d ch loop on edge of 1st section. For the upper loop, fasten in 6th ch loop, ch 28, turn, 1 dc in each st, turn, 1 dc in each dc, and fasten in 9th ch loop on opposite section.

Cut a piece of the net the exact shape of leaf, marking around the sections, catch down neatly on wrong side, and outline the veins with chain-stitch.

These leaves are also very pretty used as a border for curtains or bedspread.

COVER FOR PIANO-STOOL.

FIRST PRIZE ARTICLE.

[Contributed by Mrs. A. W. STRATTON, Framingham, Mass.]

Materials: 1-2 yard waffle or honeycomb canvas, and 2 skeins Barbour's flax embroidery thread, size oo, shade 57, or any other preferred. Use a worsted needle sufficiently large to carry the thread without fraying.

Beginning 1 1-4 inches from the edge of square, make 3 rows of darning stitch — which is merely the ordinary running stitch — around the canvas.

Commence at one corner, count in toward the centre 9 squares, bring your needle up through, make a long chain-stitch back toward the corner covering 4 squares. Push the needle down a little beyond the point of loop, and repeat this petal to form 8. Then bring the needle up through the middle of the "daisy," which is thus completed, make a French knot, and proceed with the next.

Make a row of daisies all around the edge, then make an extra one in each corner. In the cen-

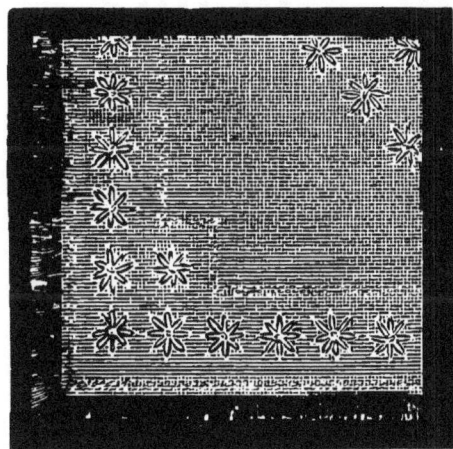

Piano-Stool Cover.

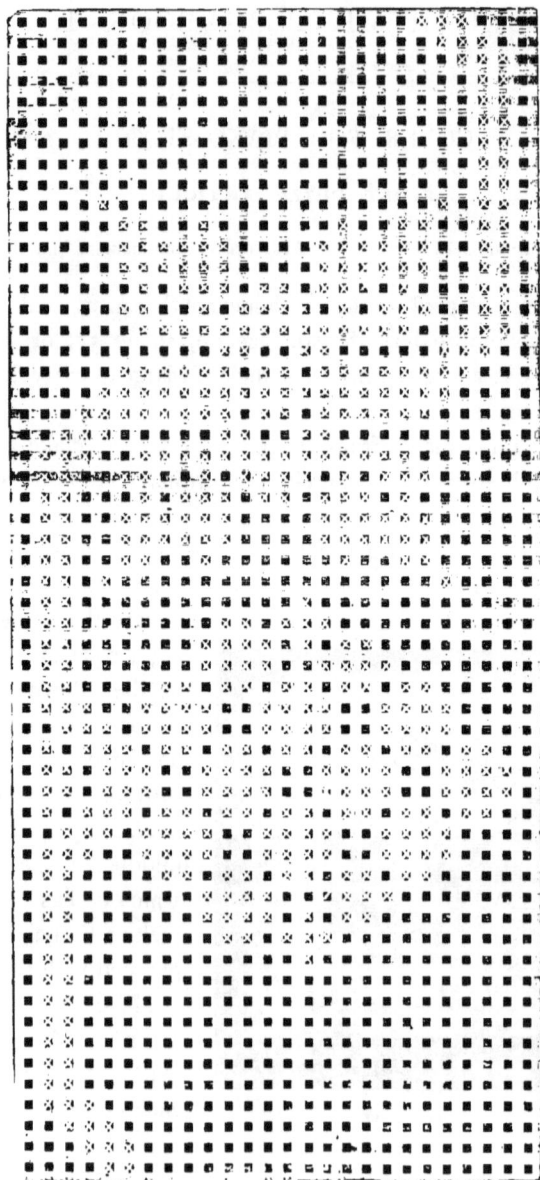

Pattern in Cross-Stitch, for Ginghams.

tre between these make a tiny star. Inside this row make another
run of darning-stitch similar to that on the outside, and in the centre
make a square of the daisies, with 1 in the midde.

The work is very rapidly done, is showy, and inexpensive, not
costing more than 25 cents to 50 cents for all materials. The flax
embroidery thread has all the lustrous beauty of silk without the cost
of the latter, and is to be preferred greatly to wool for such work as
this. If liked, the centre knot of each daisy may be made of shade
72, which is a rich brown, to simulate the real flower.

PATTERN IN CROSS–STITCH, FOR GINGHAMS.

SECOND PRIZE ARTICLE.

[Contributed by Miss SUSIE E. PRATT, East Weymouth, Mass.]

Use Barbour's linen floss, white, size aa, and a sewing-needle
large enough to carry the thread without fraying. Do not take too
long a needleful at a time, as it wears the floss to be so repeatedly
pulled through the cloth.

Choose a fine gingham, as the pattern looks much prettier on this,
and it is hardly profitable to work the coarser kinds. Work over
the dark squares, as shown by the illustration.

The two designs alternate, the diamond reversing every other
time.

DEPARTMENT 9.—BOOK 1.

EMBROIDERY SPRAY.

FIRST PRIZE ARTICLE.

[Contributed by Mrs. JAMES E. BURGESS, Madison, Wis.]

Materials: 1 skein each of Barbour's flax embroidery thread, size 8, shades 50, 57, 63, 69, and 80; a needle large enough to carry the thread without fraying; a square of pale blue twilled silk, and the same of pink lining-silk, if intended for a glove or handkerchief sachet. The material for working on should be chosen with reference to the use for which the embroidered piece is designed.

The spray is worked in satin, outline, and French-knot stitches, and is quickly executed. Trace the design lightly. Beginning with the outer edge of the roses, work a row of irregular stitches, extending toward the centre, with shade 80; then with the darker pink, shade 63, fill in from the centre, letting the stitches

Embroidery Spray.

fill in between those first made. In the centre work a little cluster
of French knots with yellow, shade 5 7, taking several long stitches
with this out from the centre, and ending with a French knot. The
outer edges of the large leaves are worked in the same way as the
roses, with the lighter green, shade 50, and filled in from the centre
with shade 69. The sepals of the roses are also worked in this shade,
with which also the outlining of the stems and centre veins of the
large leaves is done.

The possession of a color-card of Barbour's flax embroidery threads
opens a large range of possibilities to the lover of fancy work.
These flosses adapt themselves as beautifully to Kensington embroidery as to outlining, etc., and — having work which has been washed
many times — I find the colors perfectly fast. Wash them in cold
water to which a little borax is added.

LEAF DOILY.

SECOND PRIZE ARTICLE.

[Contributed by Miss SUSAN H. MANN, Greenfield, Mass.]

Materials: fine butcher's linen and Barbour's flax embroidery
thread, white, size 8.

If one has a suitable pattern, the design may be stamped lightly ; if
not, cut a paper pattern of a perfect natural leaf, mark on the linen
a circle about 8 inches in diameter, which is the size of the doily
when completed, and, using your pattern, trace a wreath of leaves
around it, the outer points touching the circle. The illustration will
show exactly how this is done. The plain centre of the doily is
from 3 1-2 to 4 inches in diameter.

After the tracing is done, work all around the edge of each leaf in
" one, two, three " stitch, which is an uneven buttonhole stitch, taking the stitches close together, and as evenly as possible at the edge.
After a little practice this work can be very rapidly executed, and is
extremely effective. The veining of the leaves is done in outline

stitch, described in No. 1 of Barbour's Prize Needlework Series, and the stems in the same way.

There are 6 doilies in the set, and each may have a different leaf-pattern. They are lovely worked with two threads of the white floss, or the colored embroidery thread may be substituted, if pre-

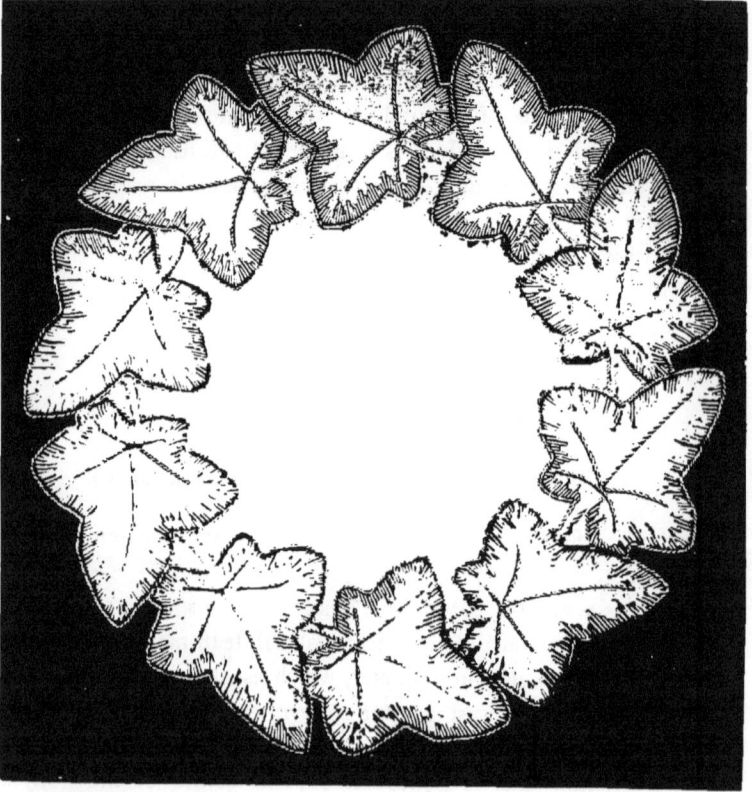

Leaf Doily.

ferred. Doilies forming a single large leaf or flower, worked in size 60 of the white flax embroidery thread, are very pretty. After the buttonhole stitching is done, cut around the outside edges carefully, being care not to clip the work.

CUSHION-COVER IN OLD ENGLISH POINT.

FIRST PRIZE ARTICLE.

[Contributed by Miss ANNA E. CONVERSE, So. Worthington, Mass.]

The beautiful work known as " Old English Point " is now quite popular, being much used in decorating table linen, etc. It is made on the same principle as the fine French point, except that

Cushion Cover in Old English Point.

heavier materials are used, consisting of braid and thread. The work is done with a common sewing-needle large enough to carry the thread.

The braid used in making the doily or cushion-cover illustrated is ⅓ inch wide, with an open-work edge on each side ; it is worked with Barbour's flax thread, white, No. 30, 3-cord, 200-yards spools.

The design is first traced on a foundation, then the braid is basted upon this, bringing all curves into shape by whipping them with fine thread. The centre and open spaces are then filled with various stitches, such as the buttonhole bar, with picots, back-stitch wheel, crown, and buttonhole lace stitches, all of which are very simple, and can easily be taken from illustration. Other stitches may be substituted, as preferred, the object being to fill the blocks effectively.

The work is really wrong side out while in progress, so it will not show its true beauty until removed from the design.

IDEAL EMBROIDERY.

SECOND PRIZE ARTICLE.

[Contributed by Miss JENNIE M. PHIPPS, Stanton, Mich.]

This beautiful lace is worked entirely with Barbour's Irish linen floss, No. aa ; other materials required are linen lawn, and one row of braid for heading.

Stamp or trace lightly with pencil the design on the lawn. Then sew around the edge of each leaf and rose, by overcasting in upper stitches of medium length, but short under stitches, a strong thread, to give a "sure foundation." Do not break the foundation thread from the spool until the entire design has been traced, thus avoiding unnecessary knots. After the foundation is thus finished, embroider in simple buttonhole stitch, drawing each stitch firm and evenly, but avoiding puckering the lawn through which you are working. In the centre of each rose is a sorrento wheel, made by crossing the threads, and working around them in the centre. The petals are filled in with a simple lace stitch, made by knotting or catching one thread into another, varying the work in different petals. In

filling in roses and leaves, pass needle through the inner edge of embroidery, under foundation thread and through the lawn only directly underneath the embroidery.

Some may desire more explicit instructions concerning the "filling-in" stitches : The rose-petal nearest the stem is filled in with "point de Bruxells," simply a succession of buttonhole stitches caught one into another. The next is filled with "point d'-Alen;" work a row of buttonhole stitches, 7 or 8, around the inner edge of petal, then pass the needle through each loop thus made, as in over-cast-

Ideal Embroidery.

ing, draw together until only a tiny hole remains in the centre, run thread down 1 stitch, pass needle through embroidery, and fasten on wrong side. Alternate these stitches in petals the entire round. The 2 inner petals are filled with twisted threads, or herringbone stitch, which needs no description. The Sorrento wheel, in centre, is made by crossing 3 threads or bars from side to side, at about equal distances, twist working thread down last bar to central point, fasten with buttonhole stitch, then work over and under the bars till the knot, or wheel, is of required size, twist thread down another bar, and fasten on wrong side.

The lower leaf, joining rose, is worked in "point d'Anvers." Fasten thread at tip of leaf, * pass downward, catch in edge of embroidery a trifle to one side of top of stem, twist back, and fasten; repeat from *, then weave in and out, from right to left, and left to right, down to 1st veins; make these in same way, and so continue down the stem. Other leaves, save the larger ones just above each rose, are filled in with sorrento bars. Fasten thread at bottom of leaf, pass upward, fasten at tip; twist down three times, catch into edge of leaf, and fasten with buttonhole stitch; the veinings are made also of twisted bars, carried up and back from main stem. The larger leaves are filled with herringbone stitch, one thread passed down the centre, and then worked across, over and under.

The "Raleigh bars," which serve to connect the pattern, are worked over a foundation or network of threads, in simple buttonhole stitch. Insert the needle in last stitch where picot is desired, twist the thread around needle 12 times, and carefully draw together, as in tatting.

When completed, the lawn is cut away, leaving the embroidery. Narrow braids may be used, if preferred, instead of working solid embroidery.

With this work, in colored embroidery threads, beautiful centre strips for table-scarfs may be made, as well as a large variety of decorations.

CUT-WORK.

[Contributed by Mrs. C. H. LAWRENCE, Morris, N.Y.]

This variety of embroidery, which is used a great deal in decoration, is done on fine linen with Barbour's flax embroidery thread, size oo. For finer work, Barbour's linen floss, size aa, or other size suitable to the work, should be chosen. For the " Sorrento " pillow-tops, which come stamped in colors for working, size oo is just the thing, and comes in all shades.

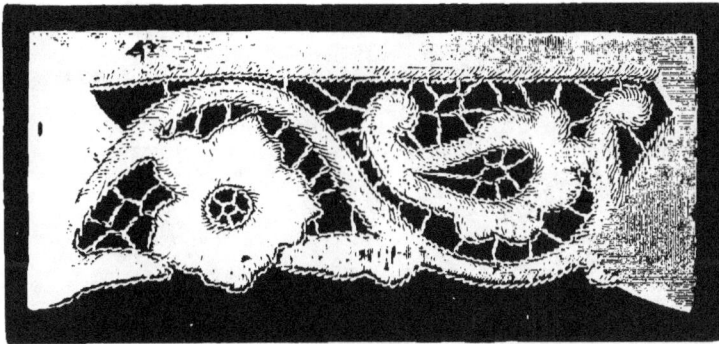

Cut-Work.

In cut-work, or Roman embroidery, the design is first stamped or traced, then outlined in close buttonhole-stitch. The bars are worked by crossing the thread from one edge to the other, twisting the thread around the bar thus formed, in returning, then working to the next bar in close buttonhole-stitch, and repeating the operation. This makes the work neater than to leave the bars until the outlining in buttonhole-stitch is completed.

When finished, cut away the material at the outlining, on the wrong side.

HONITON LACE.

[Contributed by Miss LILLIAN S. CONVERSE, So. Worthington, Mass.]

This pretty lace deserves to be better known than it is, so easily it is made, and so nice for many purposes. In the sample shown, leaf or medallion braid was used, with a plain braid and picot edge. The design is first traced on a foundation, which may easily be done by means of tracing-paper, and then the braids are basted in place, being drawn in on one edge to form the curves, and caught together

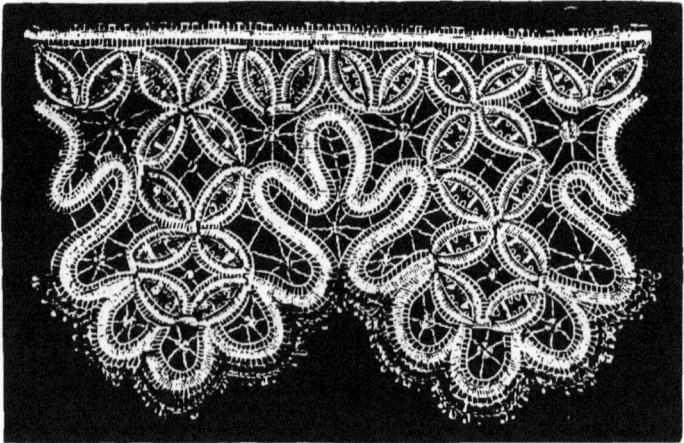

Honiton Lace.

where necessary. The open spaces are then filled in by passing twisted bars of thread across, more or less in number according to size of space, the central point of intersection being darned by weaving the thread around, over and under the bars. Narrow spaces need only the bars across.

Much latitude is given one's fancy in this work, which is adaptable to a great variety of uses. Either the white embroidery flax thread, size 8, may be used for it, or Barbour's No. 100, 3-cord, 200-yards spool linen. For coarser braids or work, coarser thread should be chosen, care being taken to use a sewing-needle that will carry it without fraying.

DRAWN–WORK DOILY.

[Contributed by Miss SUSAN H. MANN, Greenfield, Mass.]

Materials : a piece of fine linen 10 ½ inches square, and Barbour's flax thread, white, No. 100, 3-cord, 200-yards spool.

Leave for fringe 1¼ inches around the edge ; draw 3 threads across, leave ¼ inch ; draw 3 more threads, and leave ½ inch plain. Draw threads ¾ inch wide for the open-work, leave open square corners.

Hem-stitch both sides by taking up 4 threads. Buttonhole-stitch raw edges. Begin the drawn-work by tying 3 groups of threads ⅓ of the way from top, then tie ⅔ the way down this cluster of 3, and 3 more ; bring thread up and tie 3 of this last cluster and 3 new ones ; continue in this way across.

Fasten thread in buttonhole-work at corner, cross up to cluster of 3, tie each group, cross down to coarse group, tie that, tie the 2d cluster of 6, 2 together, 3 times, go up, tie coarse group, and tie each group in 3d cluster of 6, on top ; repeat across, and fasten in buttonhole-work.

Next row, fasten thread in buttonhole, tie each group in cluster of 3, cross down, tie coarse group, tie each group in 2d cluster of 6 at bottom, cross up, and tie each group in 3d cluster at top ; repeat across.

Next row, fasten thread in buttonhole-work, go up to cluster of 3, tie 2 together, then tie one group, cross down, tie coarse group, tie each group in cluster of 6 at bottom, cross up, and tie 2 together 3 times in 3d cluster of 6 at top. Repeat across ; fasten in button-hole-work.

Do the other rows in the same way, tying each loose thread as you cross it.

For the corners there must be 36 threads crossing each other;
tie together in the centre, take 4 threads, darn them back and forth
for ¼ inch, run your thread back on the under side and darn
4 more. Do this all round. For short spoke, take 2 threads of 1

Drawn-work Doily.

long spoke and 2 of next long spoke, darn these back and forth for
¼ inch, then go around and tie each loose thread.

Feather-stitch the half-inch space and briar-stitch the narrow
space; this holds the fringe   These stitches are prettier if done in
Barbour's flax embroidery thread, size 8, white. Draw threads for
fringe after the other work is completed.

This is one of the daintiest doilies that can be imagined, and has
been universally admired

CHAIR–BACK.

FIRST PRIZE ARTICLE.

[Contributed by Mrs. J. H. WHITE, St. Augustine, Fla.]

Materials: Barbour's gray flax thread, in balls, No. 16, 5-cord, and a small macramé hook.

Make a chain of 25 sts, turn.

1. Sh of 3 dtc (thread over twice), 2 ch, and 3 dtc in 5th st of ch, miss 2, 1 dtc in each of next 3 sts, ch 9, miss 9, 1 dtc in each of next 3 sts, miss 2, sh in next st, turn.

2. Ch 4, sh in sh, dtc on each of 3 dtc of last row, ch 9, 1 dtc on each of next 3 dtc, sh in sh, 1 dtc under ch of 4 at end of sh, turn.

3. Ch 4, sh in sh, 3 dtc on 3 dtc, ch 4, dc into 5th st of 9 ch in 1st row, over 9 ch in 2d row, ch 4, 3 dtc in 3 dtc, sh in sh, turn.

4. Like 2d row.

5. Like 3d row, making 9 ch instead of fastening.

6. Like 2d row.

7. Like 3d row, fasten 3 ch in a cluster, as before, letting a single ch go free. These single chs alternate with the clusters, the ribbon being passed around under the clusters and over the single chs.

When you have a strip long enough to extend around the chair, turn at the end of last row, crochet the ends together, taking care not to draw the thread too tightly, and crochet across the top, which is the side of strip in which the dtc is worked under 4 ch, thus making a continuous connection between shells. Finish the lower edge with a row of large scallops, putting 14 dtc under each ch of 4 connecting shells, and fastening down with 1 dc between the shells not

connected. Tie in a fringe, made as follows: Take a strip of
pasteboard 12 inches long, wind the flax thread over it lengthwise 6
times, slip off the loops, double in the middle, pull this loop (using
your crochet-hook) through the scallop, between middle dtc, pull
the ends of thread through the loop and draw up. Repeat this in
every scallop, and clip the ends of fringe evenly.

Take 1¾ yards of 2-inch ribbon, run in the spaces, having the
ends come in middle of front, and tie in a pretty bow.

Macramé Chair-Back.

I am sure every one who uses one of these chair-backs will prefer
it to the common "tidy." The linen macramé, too, works beautifully for such articles, having a heavy, silken appearance which in
itself is ornamental. Such a chair-back, crocheted of Barbour's colored flax thread (embroidery), size o, would be lovely. In either
case a cushion may be crocheted to match, the lining being of the
same shade as the ribbon in the back. The macramé would, of
course, be more durable, as it really improves with age, coming
from the laundry without diminished beauty.

This design may be used for a lambrequin, if liked.

SHOPPING–BAG.

SECOND PRIZE ARTICLE.

[Contributed by Miss JULIA D. SMITH, West Medway, Mass.]

Materials: Barbour's gray flax thread in balls, No. 16, 5-cord, bone hook of medium size, and silk, satine, or other preferred material for the bag, and lining for same.

Ch 49, turn.

1. Miss 4 sts, 1 dtc in each of next 3, miss 2, sh of 3 dtc, 2 ch and dtc in next st, miss 2, 1 dtc in next, * ch 2, miss 2, 1 dtc in next, repeat 3 times, 3 dtc in next 3 sts, ch 2, miss 2, 4 dtc in next 4, * ch 2, miss 2, 1 dtc in next, repeat 3 times, miss 2, sh in next st, miss 2, 4 dtc in last 4 sts, ch 4, turn.

2. 3 dtc on next 3 dtc, sh in sh, dtc on next dtc, * ch 2, dtc on next dtc, repeat twice, 3 dtc in next 3 sts, ch 4, 1 extra dtc (thread over 3 times) under 2 ch between groups of dtc, ch 4, miss 3 dtc, 4 dtc in next 4 sts, * ch 2, dtc on next dtc, repeat twice, sh in sh, 4 dtc on last 4 dtc, ch 4, turn.

3. 3 dtc on next 3 dtc (4 ch taking place of 1st), sh in sh, dtc on next 3 dtc, ch 2, dtc on next dtc, ch 2, miss 2, 4 dtc in next 4, ch 6, 3 stc (like tc except that the thread is drawn through all 3 sts at once) in last of 4 ch, top of extra dtc, and 1st of next 4 ch, ch 6, miss 3 dtc of last row, 4 dtc in next 4 sts, ch 2, 1 dtc in next dtc, ch 2, 1 dtc in next dtc, sh in sh, 4 dtc on last 4 dtc, ch 4, turn.

4. 3 dtc on next 3 dtc, sh in sh, dtc on next dtc, ch 2, miss 2, 4 dtc on next 4 sts, ch 7, 5 stc over 3 stc and 1 st on each side, ch 7, miss 3 dtc, 4 dtc in next 4 sts, ch 2, dtc on next dtc, sh in sh, 4 dtc on last 4 dtc, ch 4, turn.

5. 3 dtc on next 3 dtc, sh in sh, dtc on next dtc, ch 2, dtc on next dtc, ch 2, miss 2, 4 dtc on next 4 sts, ch 6, 3 stc in centre of 5

stc, ch 6, 3 dtc in last sts of ch and 1st of dtc following, * ch 2, miss 2, dtc in next, repeat once, sh in sh, 4 dtc on last 4 dtc, ch 4, turn.

6. 3 dtc on next 3 dtc, sh in sh, dtc on next dtc, * ch 2, dtc on next dtc, repeat twice, 3 dtc on next 3 sts, ch 4, 1 extra dtc in centre of 3 stc, ch 4, 4 dtc in last sts of ch and 1st of dtc following, * ch 2, miss 2, 1 dtc in next, repeat twice, sh in sh, 4 dtc on last 4 dtc, ch 4, turn.

Macramé Bag.

7. 3 dtc on next 3 dtc, sh in sh, dtc on next dtc, * ch 2, dtc on next dtc, repeat 3 times, 3 dtc in next 3 sts, ch 2, miss 3, 4 dtc in next 4 sts, * ch 2, miss 2, 1 dtc in next, repeat 3 times, sh in sh, 4 dtc on last 4 dtc, ch 4, turn.

8. 3 dtc on next 3 dtc, sh in sh, dtc on dtc, * ch 2, dtc on next dtc, repeat 4 times, 3 dtc in next 3 sts, * ch 2, miss 2, dtc on next dtc, repeat 4 times, sh in sh, 4 dtc on last 4 dtc, ch 4, turn.

9. 3 dtc on next 3 dtc, sh in sh, dtc on next dtc, * ch 2, dtc on next dtc, repeat 3 times, 3 dtc in next 3 sts, ch 2, miss 2, 4 dtc in next 4 sts, * ch 2, 1 dtc in next dtc, repeat 3 times, sh in sh, 4 dtc on last 4 dtc, ch 4, turn.

Repeat the pattern twice from 2d row, forming 3 diamonds. At end of last row, which will be the 7th of pattern, turn, ch 2, make a sh of 8 dtc in space between 4 dtc and sh of previous row, fasten with 1 dc in sh, sh of 8 dtc in next sp, fasten in next dtc, missing 1 sp, miss next sp, sh in next, miss next, fasten in 1st of 4 dtc, sh in next sp, fasten in last of 4 dtc, miss sp, sh in next, fasten in next dtc, missing a sp, miss next sp, sh in next, fasten in sh, sh in next sp, and fasten in end dtc, breaking the thread. Finish the other end of strip in the same way.

Cut a piece of very stiff lining canvas just the size of the strip. Prepare outside and lining of the bag (which may be made larger or smaller, as desired) ; in the model it is, when completed, 12 inches wide and 16 inches long. Catch the canvas in the centre of the lining, on the wrong side, so that it will come between lining and outside, seam the bag together, make 2 narrow runs at the top, for drawing cords, leaving 1 ¼-inch heading, make the cords of the flax macramé each a ch about 30 inches long, and run in so that one will draw out at each side of bag. To make the handles, measure from 1 to 2 yards of the macramé, according to length of handle wanted, double 6 times, cut off, pull doubled end (in which is no cut end) through between 2d and 3d shs at top, draw the other end through the loop, then using a large hook, ch the doubled thread and fasten between 5th and 6th shs. Repeat on other side. Then place the macramé strip exactly over the canvas and catch to the outside of bag, through canvas and all, with No. 50 flax thread which will be found very strong.

The sides of the bag can be pleated slightly, if desired, and any pattern may be used for the strip. One made entirely of the knot-stitch described and illustrated on page 22, Barbour's Prize Series, No. 1, is very pretty.

DEPARTMENT 12.—BOOK 1.

WHAT TO DO WITH THE FLAX THREADS.

FIRST PRIZE ARTICLE.

[Contributed by Mrs. LIZZIE ANTHONY, Oroville, Cal.]

A pretty and inexpensive bedspread can be made from one of the cheap "honeycomb" spreads. Select one that has a good central figure, surrounded by the honeycomb pattern. Outline the figure heavily with short and long buttonhole stitches, then darn the honeycomb as much or as little as you choose. Barbour's flax embroidery thread, size o, is exactly the right size for this, and shade 5 7, a sunshiny yellow, a beautiful color. If there are corner figures, they also should be outlined.

A second spread lately seen was made of cream "Holly-wood" drapery, long enough to go up under the pillows and turn forward over them, taking the place of shams. The edge of the part turned over was trimmed with crochet lace, made of No. 60 écru flax thread, 3-cord, 200-yards spools. Any pattern may be used, and 3 inches is a good, width; the prettiest pattern I have seen for this, although rather wider than necessary, is the beautiful antique lace with corner turned, given on page 17 of Barbour's Prize Needlework Series, No. 1. Sew this lace to turned-over end, and embroider or outline a handsome border above it, either a running design of poppies, terminating the curved stems, or in upright, growing position. For the poppies use flax embroidery threads, size oo (or size 8, if very fine embroidery is desired), in shades of pink (63, 67, and 80) for the poppies, and in soft olive-greens (shades 50, 51, and 94) for the leaves. If colors are not liked, a design may be etched in cream-

color or pale yellow (shade 57 or 81, size 0). This design worked
on the cream tapestry cloth, or on Bolton sheeting, which is two yards
wide and inexpensive, is very handsome.   If desired, the lace edge
can be carried entirely around the spread, in which case the latter is
not tucked in, but allowed to fall over the sides of the bed.

A dainty pair of pillow-shams may be made of 4 squares of cream
or white linen with double hemstitched hems — or plain hems with
herringbone or featherstitched edge, each square being ornamented
with an outlined design of roses ; in one may be a spray, in another a
few loose roses, etc., or any preferred design may be used.   The
squares are joined by wide crocheted or knitted insertion, made of No.
100 flax thread, either écru or white, to match the linen squares, and
the whole is edged with a lace matching the insertion.   Bureau-scarfs
and a variety of similar articles may be made in the same way, and
some may prefer to purchase hemstitched linen handkerchiefs instead
of making the squares.

A beautiful apron is made of fine black sateen with deep hem
featherstitched in dark, dull red (shade 52).   Above the hem is
worked a design of carnation pinks, in shades of pink and dull red,
the leaves of olive-green, in soft, dark shades.   (Every dealer
should have one of Barbour's color cards, from which you will
always be able to select just the sizes and shades of embroidery
flax threads suited to your work).   The apron has a pointed
bodice at top, featherstitched around the point and across the top,
ties featherstitched, with a tiny design of the pinks at the end of
each, and the edge is finished with the " knot lace " described on
page 22 of No. 1, made of black flax thread, No. 80, 3-cord, 200-
yards spools.

For a handsome tablecloth, buy the best linen sheeting, make a
wide hemstitched hem, and above this embroider a design of tulips
with white embroidery floss, size aa.   Make napkins of the same
linen, ¾ yard square, and embroider to match, making the tulip
design smaller.

A beautiful dinner set was lately made of linen Bolton sheeting ;
the hemstitched hem was 2½ inches wide, and above this was

a running vine of English ivy, worked with the white floss. Another spread had smilax instead of ivy, worked with same floss. The napkins had hems 2 inches wide, and were ⅞ yard square, with design to match the cloth worked on them. A large monogram was worked in one corner of the cloth, and a smaller one in each napkin.

A pretty trimming for children's low-neck aprons is had by working a simple cross-stitch design on the straight piece that forms the front and back yoke, and the same design on the shoulder bands. Use the linen embroidery floss. It gives a plain apron a very neat, dainty appearance to featherstitch the hems and tucks, finishing the yokes and bands in the same way. I recently finished a little dress which is very pretty. I selected a darned net pattern similar to that on page 63 of No. 1, darned 3 strips for the front and 2 for the back of waist, and a strip for the skirt about 2 yards long. A narrow pattern was worked for the neck and sleeve ruffles, and a wide one for the bottom of dress. The waist was made of clusters of fine tucks with the insertion between the clusters. The skirt had a wide ruffle with 2 clusters of tucks and the insertion between. The sleeves were made of a piece of the cloth that had been tucked in fine clusters, cut full, and gathered into bands at the wrists.

Another dress was made entirely of net, the skirt of a flounce with deep, pointed scallops, buttonhole-stitched, and darned with an "all-over" pattern — a wide insertion in the middle, then a pattern edged with a narrow scroll design, after which the wide pattern again. Any preferred design may be chosen for this. The sleeves were cut from a piece darned in the same way, the wrists finished with a narrow ruffle. It was worn over a slip of blue sateen.

A handsome tidy or cushion-cover was made of the wash-net embroidered in colored flax threads. The design was of 3 large and 3 small fans, connected by a simple scroll-pattern. The fans were worked in Oriental colors, one small fan being of pale-blue and orange, another of old-rose and yellow, and the third of peacock-blue and crimson, while the large ones were worked respectively with pale-pink and écru, orange and pale-blue, and garnet and sulphur-yellow. The

scroll-pattern is of wood-brown, sulphur-yellow, and garnet. An
inch-wide hem had 3 rows of darning stitches, the first deep garnet,
the second bright old-rose, and the third deep orange.

A beautiful bedspread may be made of darned net, the edges
trimmed with a ruffle of darned lace, and laid over silesia or sateen.
Pillow-shams are made to match, or the spread made to turn over the
pillows.

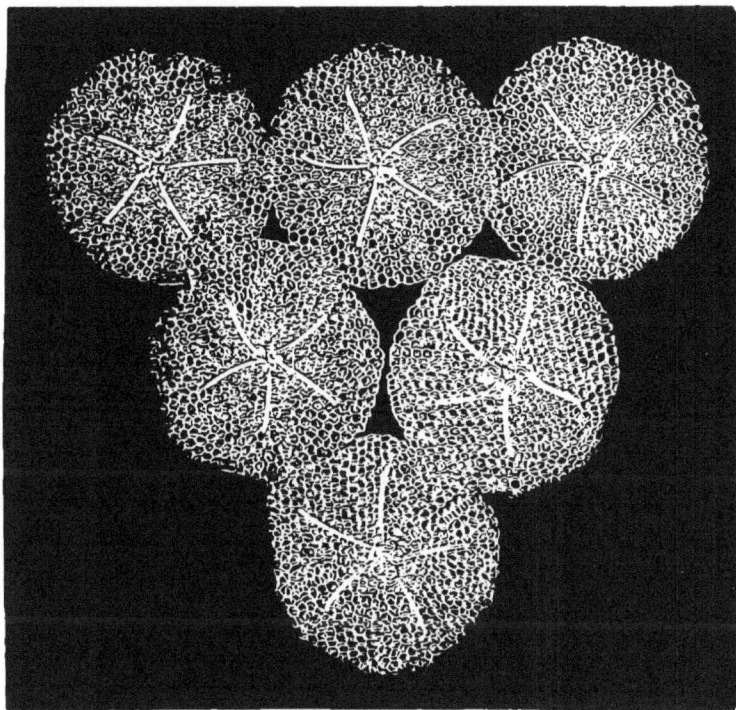

Wheels for Scarf, Cushion-Cover, etc.

A dainty table-scarf or chair-scarf is made of net darned with
cream flax thread, size oo or size 8, according to the size of mesh. A
large mesh is preferred, with size oo. Darn with an all-over design,
finish one end with a ruffle of the net with buttonhole-stitched edge,
and the other with wheels made of the net and arranged in points.
One lately seen had 2 deep points, 7 wheels in first row, 6 in 2d row,

5 in 3d, and so on down to 1 wheel.   The wheels are made by cutting a circular piece of net about 4 inches in diameter, gathering
around the edge, and drawing up closely over the centre of the circle.
Thread a needle with flax embroidery thread, size oo, pass it up
through the centre, make a French knot-stitch (page 77 of No. 1),
pushing the needle back through the wheel.   Bring it up again about
⅓ inch from outer edge of wheel, back to centre, up again, and
make another knot-stitch.   Repeat until 5 long stitches are made,
taking care to have them of equal distance apart, and same distance
from edge.   Another scarf had a row of the wheels joined and used
as insertion at each end, the hems featherstitched, and the wheels
made into a large point at one end and 2 smaller points at the other.
The hemstitching was done with yellow flax thread, shade 57, and the
centres of wheels worked with same thread.   I have seen whole
bureau-scarfs made of these wheels, with toilet-mats and cushion-
cover to match.   A great variety of uses will suggest themselves
to the worker.   For more common use, where white would soil too
quickly, the colored cheese-cloth, or Japanese scrim, may be used
for the wheels.   This comes in different delicate tints.   Or the plain
silkoline may be used.   Of course, neither of these materials is so
dainty as the net, but will bear much harder usage.

A " picture quilt " is made of either linen, sateen, or unbleached
muslin squares, any size preferred.   Each square is stamped with a
design for outlining : some choose for these all sorts of birds and
animals ; others, flower-sprays, leaves, etc. ; others prefer children's
faces and figures ; while still others have everything from a mouse to
an elephant's head.   Every square is outlined with a different color
of flax thread, and the squares are either joined and the seams covered
with fancy stitches in color, or set together with strips of knitted or
crocheted insertion of écru flax thread.   In either case the quilt or
spread is to be lined with sateen or other preferred material.

A very pretty low-neck apron, to be worn over a dark-red sateen
dress, with red silk sash, was made from gray flax thread, No. 40.   A
stiff paper pattern was first cut for the waist, with square neck and
straps over shoulders.   This was crocheted from the wheel pattern

given on page 30 of No. 1, shaping according to the paper pattern. The neck was filled in with dc, stc, tc, and dtc; above this a row of dtc separated by 2 ch, to run ribbon through, and above this row an edge of any scallop preferred. Work around the armholes in same way. The skirt has 35 wheels in each row, and for a child of three years 7 rows are required. Écru or white flax thread may be used if preferred to the gray. The apron is very handsome.

Nothing is so nice to finish the edges of infants' bands, the seams of flannel skirts, etc., as the finest size of Barbour's white embroidery floss. It washes and wears better than silk.

NETTED WINDOW–DRAPERY.

SECOND PRIZE ARTICLE.

[Contributed by Mrs. CHARLES CLEAVER, Chicago, Ill.]

Materials: Barbour's flax embroidery thread, size o, mesh 1 inch wide, and netting-needle to correspond.

This work is very simple, consisting merely of a piece of diamond-mesh netting, 25 meshes wide, and as deep as desired. Full directions for the netting have been given in Book No. 1, page 57. At the bottom, net 3 loops in 1, miss 1; in the next row, net across, and tie a tassel in each loop that was missed. The decoration consists simply of meshes, darned over and under, the threads crossing in the middle; a single row of these on each side, and 3 rows, with 2 rows of plain meshes between, at the bottom.

The use of the flax embroidery threads for making portières, draperies, sash-curtains, etc., is new to me, and I trust these hints may be the means of bringing the beautiful threads into increased use. The sample submitted is one of a pair of sash curtains, made with the flax embroidery thread, shade 57, a clear, sunny yellow, and the effect of these curtains in a north room is charming.

Size oo would be more suitable for smaller articles, drapes, etc.

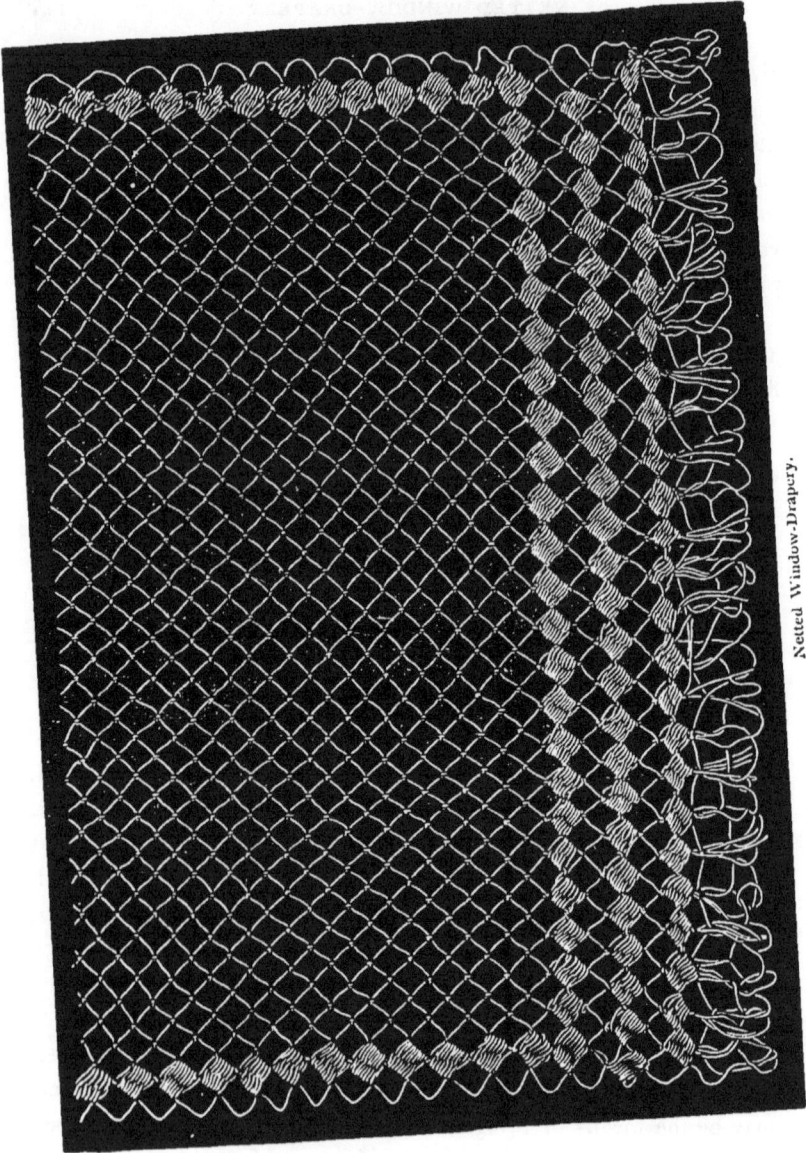

Netted Window-Drapery.

DRESS TRIMMING.

[Contributed by Mrs. JAMES E. BURGESS, Madison, Wis.]

Materials: Barbour's cream flax thread, No. 40, 3-cord, 200-yards spools, brass rings about one-half inch in diameter, beads as desired, and steel hook large enough to carry the thread nicely. String the beads on the thread.

1. Cover ring with 42 dc, fasten 1st to last dc.

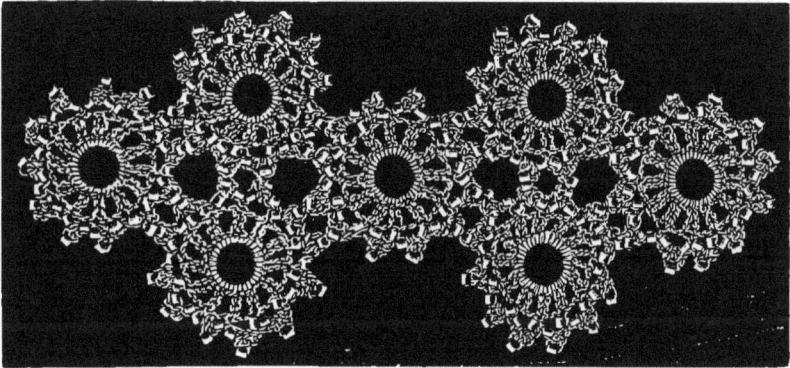

Dress Trimming.

2. Ch 3 for 1 tc, 1 tc in next st, ch 1, miss 1, 2 tc in next 2 sts, repeat around the ring, making 12 groups of 2 tc, each separated by 1 ch, fasten 1st to last.

3. Put hook in 1 ch between groups of tc, slip up bead, make 1 ch, then 1 ch without bead, 1 ch with bead, fasten between tc, and repeat all around.

4. Make 1 dc, 1 tc between beads of 3d row, 1 ch with bead, 1 tc and 1 dc between beads in 3d row; repeat.

These wheels may be put together in a great variety of patterns. The idea of using flax threads in this way is original with me, as I wished to trim a cream serge dress, and could not find such trimming as I wanted. This is easily made and very dainty.

EXPLANATION OF TERMS AND ABBREVIATIONS USED IN BARBOUR'S PRIZE NEEDLE–WORK SERIES.

TERMS USED IN KNITTING.

K, knit plain.

O, over; thread over needle, forming an extra stitch. O 2, over twice.

N, narrow; knit two stitches together.

P, purl (or seam); knit with thread before needle.

Sl, n, and b, slip, narrow, and bind; slip first stitch, narrow next two, and draw slipped stitch over.

Sl and b, slip and bind; same as sl, n, and b, omitting the narrowing. To cast or bind off, continue the process.

Stars and parentheses indicate repetition; thus, * o2, n, repeat from * twice, and (o 2, n,) 3 times, mean the same as o 2, n, o 2, n, o 2, n.

TERMS USED IN CROCHETING.

Ch, chain; a straight series of loops, each drawn with the hook through the one preceding it.

Sc, single crochet; hook through work, thread over and draw through work and stitch on hook at same time.

Dc, double crochet; hook through work, thread over, and draw through, over, and draw through two stitches on hook.

Tc, treble crochet; over, draw thread through work, over, draw through two stitches on hook, over, and draw through remaining two.

Stc, short treble crochet; like treble, save that the thread is drawn through the three stitches at once.

Dtc, double treble crochet; thread over twice before insertion of hook in work, then proceed as in treble crochet.

P, picot; a loop of chain joined by catching in first stitch of chain.

Complete illustrated directions for these stitches are given in "No. 1" of the Prize Series.

——— BARBOUR'S ———

ULSTER ROPE LINEN FLOSS

is continually and rapidly advancing in popularity as its perfect adaptability to the varied uses of expensive silks becomes more strongly attested. Its smoothness and lustre is unsurpassed. It is especially adapted for Embroidery, for the decoration of a thousand and one articles for home use and adornment, and with equally as charming effect can be applied as readily to the uses of Knotting, Netting, Knitting, Crocheting, and kindred arts. For Slippers, Mittens, Purses, etc., it is durable, lustrous, firm, and far less expensive than silk, and its sale in this new field is constantly increasing.

75 shades are now on the market, including the Newest Art Shades, and the old favorites ; others will be added as approved.

Ask your Dealer for

BARBOUR'S ULSTER ROPE LINEN FLOSS.

TO WASH EMBROIDERY.

Make a light suds with Ivory or other pure soap, and (particularly for the first laundering) cool water. Wash one article at a time, finishing with this before taking another. Do not rub the embroidery, or put soap directly upon it. Rinse carefully and quickly in clear, cold water, to which a little salt may be added. After rinsing, place between two thick towels, or in one which may be folded over, roll up, squeeze (in order to extract the moisture), then unroll, place right side down on a soft cloth or flannel folded in several thicknesses, lay a white cloth over the wrong side, and press until dry with a moderately hot iron.

Ask for Barbour's.

It is the best for all uses.

Insist upon having it.

Sold everywhere.

See that the threads you purchase bear labels similar to the following. THEY ARE STANDARD.

3-CORD 200 YARDS SPOOL THREAD.

IN

DARK BLUE, for strong Sewing.

WHITE,

WD. BROWN,
(Ecru.)

DRABS.

} For Lace Making and Needlework.

TOP LABEL.

REVERSE LABEL.

BALL THREAD.

COLORS.

GREY, WHITE & ECRU.
1 Oz. Balls.

SIZES.

NOS. 16 TO 70.
(No. 70 Fine Size.)

LINEN FLOSSES
In all the Art Shades.

BARBOUR'S STANDARD
3-Cord Carpet Thread.

TRADE FLAX MARK	ULSTER ROPE LINEN FLOSS. THE BARBOUR BROTHERS CO. NEW YORK.	SIZE 00 SHADE No 3

Size 00, "Rope," Medium.
" 4, "Etching," Fine.
White Flossette. * ** *** ****
Fine to Coarse.

IN ALL COLORS.

Ask for Barbour's.

BARBOUR'S
IRISH FLAX THREAD
TRADE MARK.
FLAX

THE BARBOUR BROTHERS COMPANY.

NEW YORK, 218 CHURCH ST.

Boston, 58 South St.   Chicago, 108 & 110 Franklin St.
Philadelphia, 410 Arch St.   Cincinnati, 118 East 6th St.
San Francisco, 517 & 519 Market St.   St. Louis, 814 Lucas Ave.

www.ingramcontent.com/pod-product-compliance
Lightning Source LLC
Chambersburg PA
CBHW030607270326
41927CB00007B/1077